Landbird Community Monitoring at Congaree National Park, 2009

Natural Resource Report NPS/SECN/NRDS—2011/306

Michael W. Byrne

USDI National Park Service
Southeast Coast Inventory and Monitoring Network
Cumberland Island National Park
101 Wheeler Street
Saint Marys, Georgia, 31558

Joseph C. DeVivo and Jennifer R. Asper

USDI National Park Service
Southeast Coast Inventory and Monitoring Network
University of Georgia
160 Phoenix Road, Phillips Lab
Athens, Georgia, 30605

and

Brent A. Blankley

USDI National Park Service
Southeast Coast Network
100 Alabama St SW
Atlanta, GA 30303

September 2011

U.S. Department of the Interior
National Park Service
Natural Resource Stewardship and Science
Fort Collins, Colorado

The National Park Service, Natural Resource Stewardship and Science office in Fort Collins, Colorado publishes a range of reports that address natural resource topics of interest and applicability to a broad audience in the National Park Service and others in natural resource management, including scientists, conservation and environmental constituencies, and the public.

The Natural Resource Data Series is intended for the timely release of basic data sets and data summaries. Care has been taken to assure accuracy of raw data values, but a thorough analysis and interpretation of the data has not been completed. Consequently, the initial analyses of data in this report are provisional and subject to change.

All manuscripts in the series receive the appropriate level of peer review to ensure that the information is scientifically credible, technically accurate, appropriately written for the intended audience, and designed and published in a professional manner. Data in this report were collected and analyzed using methods based on established, peer-reviewed protocols and were analyzed and interpreted within the guidelines of the protocols.

Views, statements, findings, conclusions, recommendations, and data in this report do not necessarily reflect views and policies of the National Park Service, U.S. Department of the Interior. Mention of trade names or commercial products does not constitute endorsement or recommendation for use by the U.S. Government.

This report is available from (http://science.nature.nps.gov/im/units/secn) and the Natural Resource Publications Management website (http://www.nature.nps.gov/publications/nrpm/).

Please cite this publication as:

Byrne, M. W., J. C. DeVivo, J. R. Asper, and B. A. Blankley. 2011. Landbird monitoring at Congaree National Park, 2009. Natural Resource Data Series NPS/SECN/NRDS—2011/306. National Park Service, Fort Collins, Colorado.

NPS 178/110323, September 2011

Contents

Contents (continued)

Figures

Tables

Executive Summary

Birds are an important component of park ecosystems, and their high body temperature, rapid metabolism, and high ecological position in most food webs make them a good indicator of the effects of local and regional changes in ecosystems. Long-term trends in the community composition, relative abundance, distribution, and occurrences of breeding-bird populations provide a measure for assessing the ecological integrity and sustainability in southeastern systems. Further, long-term patterns of these attributes in relation to changes in the structural diversity of vegetation resulting from fire and other management practices will improve our understanding of the effects of various management actions. This report summarizes data collected with the Draft SECN Landbird Community Monitoring Protocol (Byrne et al., *in preparation*) at Congaree National Park in 2009.

1. Data were collected at 32 spatially-balanced random locations at the Park using an adaptation of the variable-circular plot (VCP) technique with distance estimation.

2. Sampling activities occurred at the Park in May and June 2009.

3. We detected 1,047 birds representing 68 species.

4. No non-native species were detected.

5. Monitoring efforts resulted in the addition of one new species to the Park's official species list: barred owl.

6. An evaluation of sampling effort relative to the number of species detected indicated that the sample adequately characterized the bird diversity, and analyses suggest bird diversity is high at the Park.

7. Carolina wren and Northern cardinal were the most widely distributed species at the Park; occurring at 97% of sampling locations. Northern parula and tufted titmouse were the second-most widely distributed species at the Park, detected in 94% of sampling locations.

8. The full dataset, and associated metadata, can be acquired from the data store at http://science.nature.nps.gov/nrdata/

.

Introduction

Overview

Birds are an important component of park ecosystems, and their high body temperature, rapid metabolism, and high ecological position in most food webs make them good indicators of the effects of local and regional changes in ecosystems. It has also been suggested that management activities aimed at preserving habitat for bird populations, such as for neotropical migrants, can have the added benefit of preserving entire ecosystems and their attendant ecosystem services (Karr 1991, Maurer and Heywood 1993). Moreover, birds have a tremendous following among the public, and many parks provide information on the status and trends of birds in their park through interpretive programs.

Bird populations are affected by a variety of stressors; however, the primary agents are habitat loss and degradation. The Southeastern U.S. has a long history of documented species extinctions associated with habitat loss, degradation, and over-harvest, including the passenger pigeon, Carolina parakeet, ivory-billed woodpecker, Zenaida dove, Key West quail-dove, and dusky seaside sparrow. Analysis of both Breeding Bird Survey and Christmas Bird Count (CBC) long-term datasets indicate decreasing counts and shifting and condensed ranges of many migratory and non-migratory bird species within the last 40 years (Sauer et al. 1997, Niven et al. 2009). The last four decades of CBC data indicate a northward shift in the occurrences of 68.2% (208/305) of the species detected (Niven et al. 2009). Although several factors are associated with changes in bird populations and ranges, climate change is suspected as a causative agent (Strode 2003, Butler 2003, Marra et al. 2005, Mills 2005, Murphy-Klassen et al. 2005, Visser and Both 2005); however habitat loss and degradation are the more likely agents in the short term. Bird communities are also good indicators of ecological conditions and several bioassessment approaches have been developed using birds (Croonquist and Brooks 1991, Bradford et al. 1998, O'Connell et al. 2000, Bryce et al. 2002, Coppedge et al. 2006).

The Southeastern U.S. serves as an important migration corridor and wintering ground for many northern-breeding species and as a breeding area for resident and breeding birds. All migratory species depend on quality stopover areas, and the juxtaposition of SECN parks in the Atlantic Flyway make them important stopover areas during the spring and fall migrations and also serve as key wintering areas for several species. The SECN has over 400 known bird species (NPSpecies 2011), including several state- and federally listed species. Consequently, birds ranked high in the SECN Vital Signs selection process.

Long-term trends in the community composition, diversity, and occupancy of breeding-bird populations provide a measure for assessing the ecological integrity and sustainability in southeastern systems, and identifying the need for specific management activities on our park lands. Further, long term trends in arrival phenology will assist park managers in developing and implementing mitigation strategies in response to predicted patterns in climate change.

The National Park Service Omnibus Management Act of 1998, and other reinforcing policies and regulations, require park managers "to establish baseline information and to provide information on the long-term trends in the condition of National Park System resources" (Title II, Sec. 204). The bird-community monitoring data summarized herein is a tool to assist park managers in fulfilling this mandate.

This report summarizes data collected under the draft SECN Landbird Community Monitoring Protocol (Byrne et al., *in preparation*).

Study Area

Congaree National Park (CONG) is located in central South Carolina approximately 30km southeast of the capital city of Columbia (Figure 1). The 10,845-ha (26,800 ac) park is bordered to the south by the Congaree River and the Wateree River to the east. The Park consists of the largest contiguous bottomland-hardwood forest remaining in the United States. As such, it consists of a variety of aquatic and terrestrial community types, and, correspondingly, hosts a phenomenal diversity of flora and fauna. Because the Park is predominantly a floodplain, the vegetation communities are primarily driven by hydrologic process (i.e., hydroperiod) and soil type, and range from bald cypress (*Taxodium distichum*)- and water / swamp tupelo (*Nyssa aquatica / biflora*)- dominated communities to loblolly pine and longleaf pine (*Pinus taeda* and *P. palustris*) communities, and old pine plantations, that occur along the northern edge of the Park. The majority of the Park's vegetation communities, however, have a strong component of sugarberry (*Celtis laevigata*), sweetgum (*Liquidambar styraciflua*), and laurel oak (*Quercus laurifolia*) (American Geographic Data, Inc. 2001).

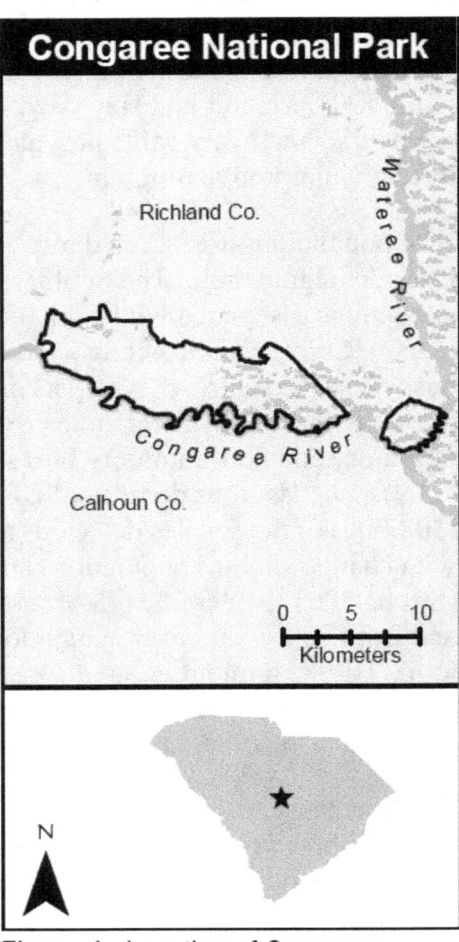

Figure 1. Location of Congaree National Park.

Due to the unique properties of the Park, it has been designated an International Biosphere Reserve, National Natural Landmark, Globally Important Bird Area, and also includes a 6075-ha (15,010 ac) congressionally-designated Wilderness Area. Further, the Park is renowned for its numerous national- and state-champion trees.

Given the location of CONG within the watershed, the park is subject to a variety of aquatic-based stressors (i.e., pollutants) from upstream sources. Further, an unmanaged feral hog population (*Sus scrofa*) occurs at the Park and causes widespread rooting and herbivory damage. The Park has an active fire-management program to restore and maintain the upland communities (i.e., those dominated by *Pinus* spp.).

CONG has 192 known bird species, including one species added to the species list because of this monitoring effort (NPSpecies 2010) (Appendix A). .

Monitoring Objective

- Determine trends in landbird-species occupancy, distribution, diversity, and community composition in SECN parks.

Methods

Sampling Design

A detailed explanation of the sampling design and site selection can be found in the SECN Draft Landbird Monitoring Protocol (Byrne et al., *in preparation*) and sample site selection SOP (Byrne 2009). In summary, to allow for park-wide inference, the CONG administrative boundary was used as the sampling frame. The sampling frame was divided into a systematic 0.5-ha grid; the center point of each grid cell served as the potential sampling site. A spatially-balanced sample was drawn from this grid using the Reversed Randomized Quadrant-Recursive Raster (RRQRR) algorithm (Theobald et al. 2007). Alternate points were used when selection criteria (i.e., including safety and access issues) were not met. A sample size of 32 was chosen after consideration of the Park's size, hypothesized variability, and logistical issues.

Sampling Methodology

We used an adaptation of variable-circular plot (VCP) technique with distance estimation (Reynolds et al. 1980, Ralph et al. 1993, Fancy 1997, Buckland et al. 1993, 2001). Bird surveys were conducted at the center point of each 0.5-ha macroplot (see Sampling Design) from April – June. This time period was selected to maximize detecting species that reproduce within the parks and also detect migratory birds. All birds observed by sight and sound were recorded. Surveys occurred from 0530 – 1100. Upon arrival at the station, all sampling event information was recorded. Sampling began five to ten minutes after arriving at the sample location to allow birds present to resume normal behaviors. Data were not collected at Beaufort wind speed codes greater than 6 (i.e., winds >24mph), as this substantially impedes detectability.

At each station, counts were separated into four time segments of equal duration, 0-3 minutes (to allow comparisons with BBS data), 3-6 minutes, 5-9 minutes, and 9-12 minutes. Distance to each bird detected was estimated and categorized into one of four distance classes (0-25m, 25-50, 50-100, >100). Birds considered flyovers were also recorded. Each sampling location was sampled two times during the sampling period, at least three weeks apart, in an effort to detect migrants or breeders that arrive at different times of the year. All detections were made via auditory cues or visual observations with binoculars.

Data Analysis

Data in this report represent one year and are summarized in three general categories: diversity, composition, and distribution. Sampling locations are presented in Figure 2, labeled locations are presented in Appendix B, and species detected at each location are presented in Appendix C. Despite a well-trained and dedicated field crew, complete identification of all individuals encountered was not always possible. Species were identified to the most refined taxonomic level possible (e.g., *Corvus*, Parulidae, Ciconiiformes).

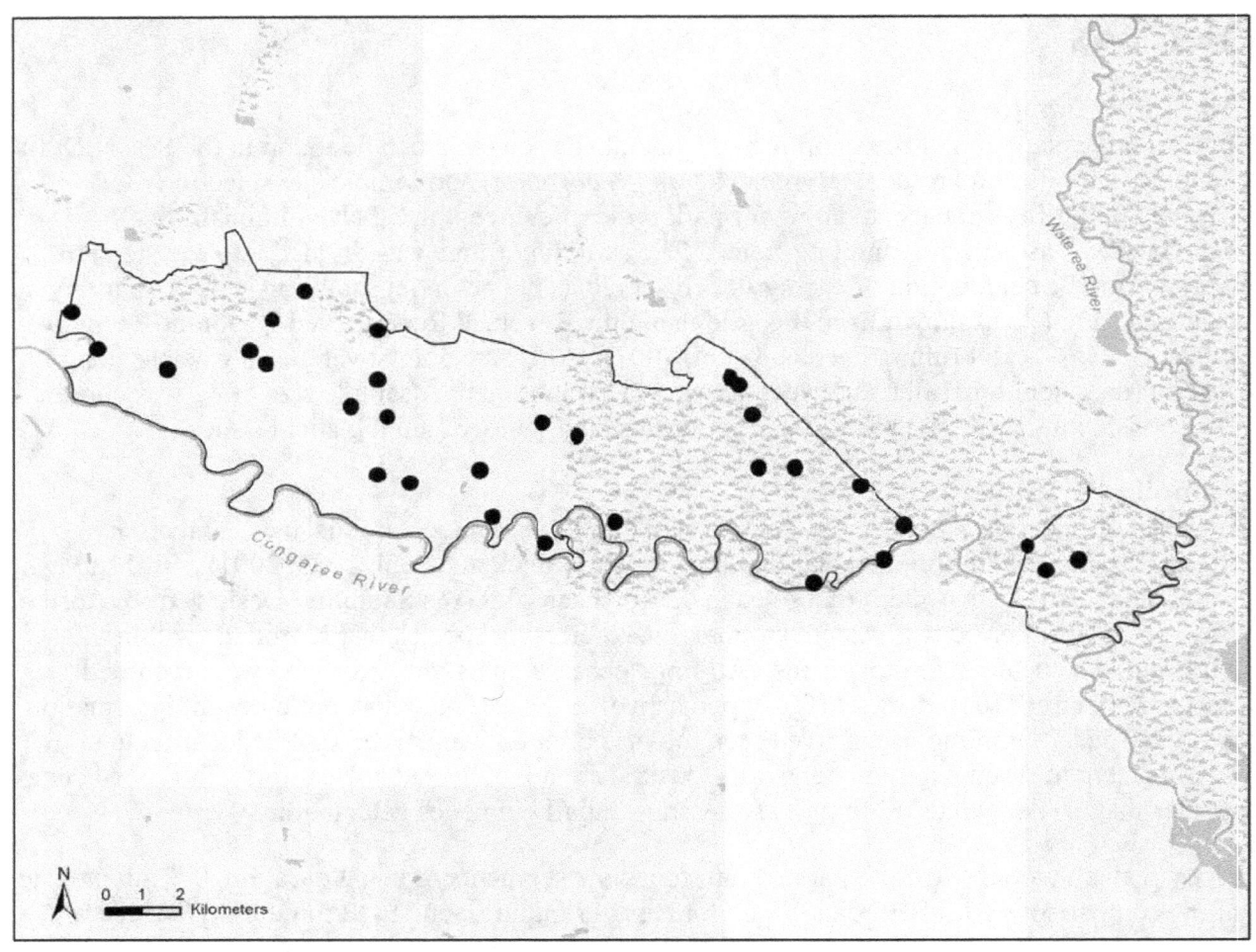

Figure 2. Spatially-balanced random sampling locations at Congaree National Park, 2009.

Composition

Measures of community composition are often good indicators of abiotic variability, disturbance, or other stressors. Summaries related to sample composition include the total number of individuals and species detected, and proportional abundances of each species in the overall sample. For all species detected we calculated the proportion of sites where the species was detected at least once. All non-native species detections were pooled to calculate the proportion of sites where at least one non-native species was detected. Summaries of composition are presented for all landbirds detected. This section also presents any new species detected and addresses the detection of any species of management concern or interest.

Distribution

Understanding changes in the distribution of bird species is integral to informed management of species and their requisite habitats. Changes in species distributions over time provide useful information at both the local and landscape scale relating to how species respond to large-scale influences such as changing land use, climate, hydrology, or habitat quality/ availability. Climate change, for example, influences the distribution, phenology, population demographics, and abundance of individual bird species. Cascading effects through altered species interactions and alterations within the web structure will also have the capacity to impact ecosystem processes (Montoya and Raffaelli 2010, USGS 2011).

Diversity

Diversity is defined as "the variety and abundance of species in a defined unit of study" (Magurran 2004, p. 8). Diversity is a community property that is related to trophic structure, productivity, stability, (McIntosh 1967, McNaughton 1977), immigration / emigration (Colwell and Lees 2000), and ecological condition (i.e., ecological integrity as defined by Karr and Chu 1995). Species diversity consists of two components: the number of species (species richness) and the relative abundance of those species (species evenness / dominance) within a defined community (Margalef 1958, Lloyd and Ghelardi 1964, Pielou 1966). Species diversity is often communicated in the form of diversity indices. The term community refers to the assemblage of species populations that occur together in space and time (Begon et al. 1986), and we consider the Park as a whole community as per the conceptual ecological models presented in our monitoring plan (see Chapter 2 in DeVivo et al. 2008).

Because diversity indices respond differently to various mechanisms that influence community change, several indices must be used to adequately characterize diversity in SECN parks (Haedrick 1975, Boyle et al. 1984). After careful appraisal of advantages and disadvantages of the many diversity indices, a suite of alpha diversity indices were selected to summarize these data (Table 1), where alpha diversity is the diversity of species within a defined area, community, or ecosystem (Whittaker 1972).

Species diversity estimates are based only on bird observations identified to the species level, as they were the primary target of this monitoring effort. Non-native birds were not included in diversity estimates.

Table 1. Diversity indices used, corresponding symbol, community attribute the index reflects, the range of index values, and notes on each index.

Index	Symbol	Community Attribute	Index Citation	Notes
Native Spp. Richness	S_{obs}	Richness	n/a	Value is a positive integer that indicates the number of native species in the sample. Intuitive. Good discriminant ability if sampling effort is comparable; sensitive to sample size, the occurrence of rare species, or those with low detectability; does not account for relative abundances.
Chao 1	**Chao1**	Richness	Chao (1984) Chao (1987)	Values indicate an estimate of species richness; abundance-based estimate; works well with dataset containing several infrequent observations[a].
Chao 2	**Chao2**	Richness	Chao (1984) Chao (1987)	Values indicate an estimate of total species richness (including species not present in the sample); incidence-based estimate; works well with dataset containing several infrequent observations[a].
Abundance-based Coverage	**ACE**	Richness	Chao and Lee (1992) Chazdon et al. (1998)	Values indicate an estimate of species richness; abundance-based estimate.
Incidence-based Coverage	**ICE**	Richness	Lee and Chao (1994) Chazdon et al. (1998)	Values indicate an estimate of total species richness (including species not present in the sample); incidence-based estimate.
Jackknife 1	**Jack1**	Richness	Burnham and Overton (1978) Burnham and Overton (1979) Heltshe and Forrester (1983)	Values indicate an estimate of total species richness (including species not present in the sample); incidence-based estimate; The higher the value the higher the species richness. This procedure requires no assumptions regarding the data distribution.
Jackknife 2	**Jack2**	Richness	Smith and van Belle (1984)	Values indicate an estimate of species richness; incidence-based estimate.
Bootstrap	**Boot**	Richness	Smith and van Belle (1984)	Values indicate an estimate of species richness; incidence-based estimate.

[a] (Chao 1984), [b] (Kempton 2002), [c] (Kempton and Taylor 1974), [d] (Hayek and Buzas 1997), [e] (Wolda 1983), [f] (Kempton and Wedderburn 1978), [g] (Magurran 1988), [h] (Lexerød and Eid 2006), [i] (Magurran 2004)

Table 1. Continued.

Index	Symbol	Community Attribute	Index Citation	Notes
Fisher's α	α	Richness	Fisher et al. (1943)	Value is a positive integer and indicates a relative estimate of species richness; good discriminant ability, low sensitivity to sample size, and robust to deviations in the assumed distribution [b, c, d, e]; abundance-based estimate.
Q Statistic	Q	Richness	Kempton and Taylor (1976) Kempton and Taylor (1978)	Value is a positive integer and indicates a relative estimate of species richness. Good discriminant ability and low bias with small samples[f], model fit is irrelevant to index performance[g]; value is not weighted towards abundant or rare species; abundance-based estimate.
Smith and Wilson	E_{var}	Evenness	Smith and Wilson (1996)	Values range from 0 (no evenness) to 1 (perfectly even and all species exists in relatively equal abundance); weighs common species more heavily than rare species (desirable in certain cases).
Smith and Wilson 1/D	$E_{1/D}$	Evenness	Smith and Wilson (1996) Simpson (1949)	Values range from 0 (no evenness) to 1 (perfectly even and all species exists in relatively equal abundance); weighs rare and abundant species equally (desirable in certain cases).
Camargo	E'	Evenness	Camargo (1992)	Values range from 0 (no evenness) to 1 (perfectly even and all species exists in relatively equal abundance); performs well estimating intermediate values of evenness than the other indices; weighs rare and abundant species equally (desirable in certain cases).
Gini	E_G	Evenness	Gini (1912)	Values range from 0 (no evenness) to 1 (perfectly even and all species exists in relatively equal abundance); Good discriminant ability and low sensitivity to sample size[h].
Berger-Parker	D_{BP}	Dominance	Berger and Parker (1970)	Values range from 0 (no single-species dominance) to 1 (sample is strongly dominated by a single species); describes the proportional dominance of the single most abundant species; low sensitivity to sample size but poor discriminant ability[i] – not used for across year or site comparisons.

[a] (Chao 1984), [b] (Kempton 2002), [c] (Kempton and Taylor 1974), [d] (Hayek and Buzas 1997), [e] (Wolda 1983), [f] (Kempton and Wedderburn 1978), [g] (Magurran 1988), [h] (Lexerød and Eid 2006), [i] (Magurran 2004)

17

Results

Composition

We detected 1,047 birds representing 68 species. The majority of the overall sample consisted of Northern parula (9.8%), Northern cardinal (8.1%), Carolina wren (7.8%), and tufted titmouse (6.7%) (Figure 3). Occupancy provides insight into the distribution of species across the park and whether a species is commonly or uncommonly encountered; however, this is strongly influenced by a species' detectability [which is affected by habitat characteristics and will be accounted for in future analyses (MacKenzie et al. 2002)] as more-easily detected species can be more frequently encountered. No species occupied all sampling locations; however Carolina wren and Northern cardinal occupied 97% of the sampling locations, and Northern parula and tufted titmouse occupied 94% of the sampling locations (Table 2). Blue-gray gnatcatcher, Acadian flycatcher, red-bellied woodpecker, red-eyed vireo, and yellow-billed cuckoo occupied approximately 80% of the locations (Table 2). No non-native species were detected.

Several species identified by Watson and Malloy (2008) as priority species were detected during this sampling effort, including: Acadian flycatcher, bald eagle, blackpoll warbler, chimney swift, Eastern kingbird, Eastern towhee, Eastern wood-pewee, great egret, hooded warbler, indigo bunting, Kentucky warbler, Louisiana waterthrush, Mississippi kite, Northern parula, orchard oriole, pine warbler, prairie warbler, prothonotary warbler, red-bellied woodpecker, red-headed woodpecker, red-shouldered hawk, solitary sandpiper, summer tanager, Swainson's warbler, white-eyed vireo, wood thrush, worm-eating warbler, yellow-billed cuckoo, yellow-throated vireo, and yellow-throated warbler.

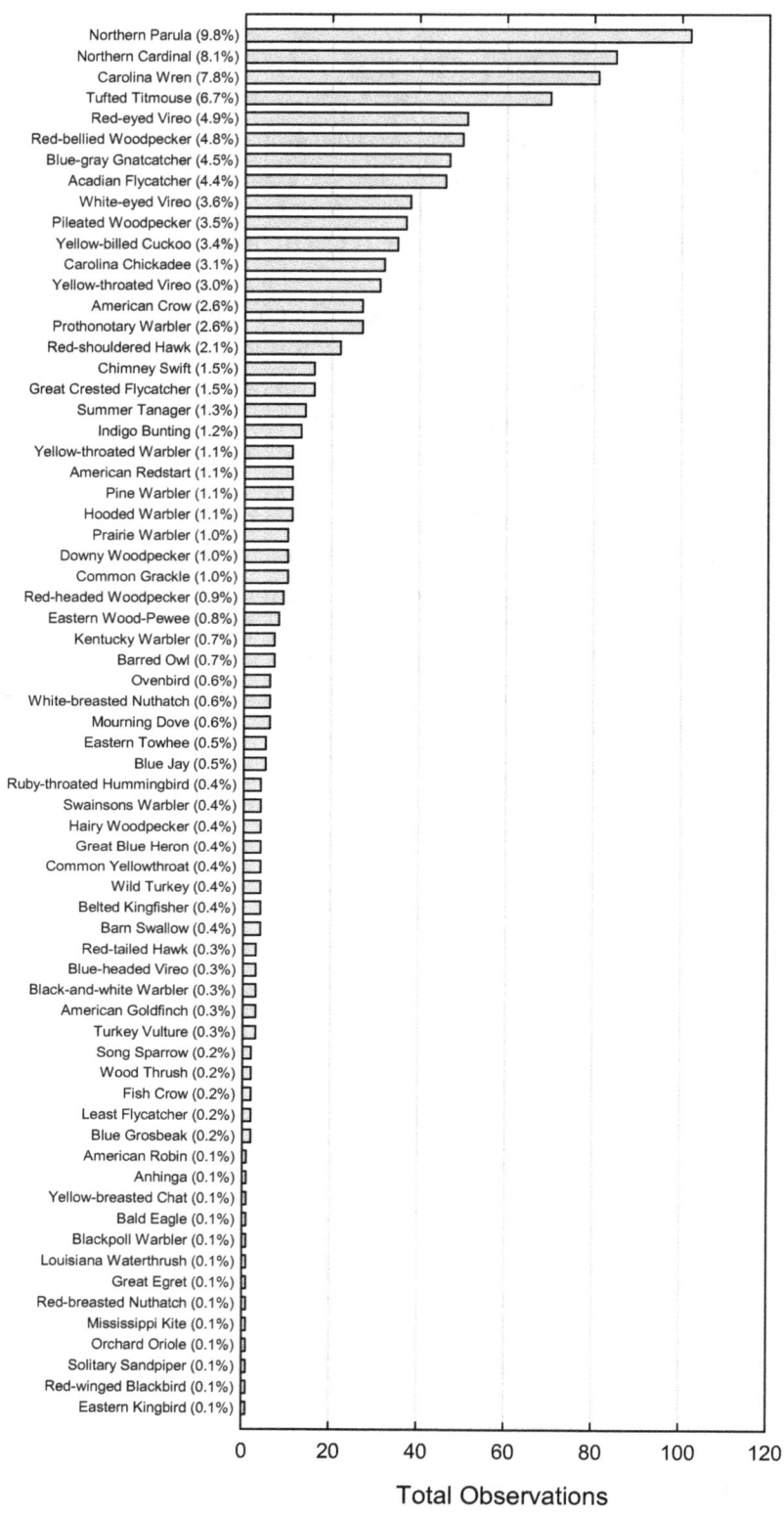

Figure 3. Proportions of bird species observed at Congaree National Park, 2009.

Table 2. Proportion of sites where each bird species was detected at Congaree National Park, 2009.

Common Name	Scientific Name	Proportion of Sites Where Observed
Carolina Wren	*Thryothorus ludovicianus*	0.97
Northern Cardinal	*Cardinalis cardinalis*	0.97
Northern Parula	*Parula americana*	0.94
Tufted Titmouse	*Baeolophus bicolor*	0.94
Blue-gray Gnatcatcher	*Polioptila caerulea*	0.81
Acadian Flycatcher	*Empidonax virescens*	0.78
Red-bellied Woodpecker	*Melanerpes carolinus*	0.78
Red-eyed Vireo	*Vireo olivaceus*	0.78
Yellow-billed Cuckoo	*Coccyzus americanus*	0.78
Pileated Woodpecker	*Dryocopus pileatus*	0.72
White-eyed Vireo	*Vireo griseus*	0.66
Carolina Chickadee	*Poecile carolinensis*	0.63
Yellow-throated Vireo	*Vireo flavifrons*	0.56
American Crow	*Corvus brachyrhynchos*	0.53
Red-shouldered Hawk	*Buteo lineatus*	0.50
Prothonotary Warbler	*Protonotaria citrea*	0.44
Great Crested Flycatcher	*Myiarchus crinitus*	0.38
Summer Tanager	*Piranga rubra*	0.34
Downy Woodpecker	*Picoides pubescens*	0.31
Indigo Bunting	*Passerina cyanea*	0.28
Yellow-throated Warbler	*Dendroica dominica*	0.28
Hooded Warbler	*Wilsonia citrina*	0.25
Barred Owl	*Strix varia*	0.22
American Redstart	*Setophaga ruticilla*	0.19
Eastern Wood-Pewee	*Contopus virens*	0.19
Blue Jay	*Cyanocitta cristata*	0.16
Chimney Swift	*Chaetura pelagica*	0.16
Common Grackle	*Quiscalus quiscula*	0.16
Ovenbird	*Seiurus aurocapillus*	0.16
Red-headed Woodpecker	*Melanerpes erythrocephalus*	0.16
White-breasted Nuthatch	*Sitta carolinensis*	0.16
Belted Kingfisher	*Megaceryle alcyon*	0.13
Great Blue Heron	*Ardea herodias*	0.13
Kentucky Warbler	*Oporornis formosus*	0.13
Pine Warbler	*Dendroica pinus*	0.13
Prairie Warbler	*Dendroica discolor*	0.13
Ruby-throated Hummingbird	*Archilochus colubris*	0.13
Wild Turkey	*Meleagris gallopavo*	0.13
American Goldfinch	*Carduelis tristis*	0.09
Black-and-white Warbler	*Mniotilta varia*	0.09
Common Yellowthroat	*Geothlypis trichas*	0.09
Eastern Towhee	*Pipilo erythrophthalmus*	0.09
Hairy Woodpecker	*Picoides villosus*	0.09

Table 2. Continued.

Common Name	Scientific Name	Proportion of Sites Where Observed
Mourning Dove	*Zenaida macroura*	0.09
Red-tailed Hawk	*Buteo jamaicensis*	0.09
Swainson's Warbler	*Limnothlypis swainsonii*	0.09
Worm-eating Warbler	*Helmitheros vermivorus*	0.09
Barn Swallow	*Hirundo rustica*	0.06
Blue Grosbeak	*Guiraca caerulea*	0.06
Blue-headed Vireo	*Vireo solitarius*	0.06
Fish Crow	*Corvus ossifragus*	0.06
Song Sparrow	*Melospiza melodia*	0.06
Turkey Vulture	*Cathartes aura*	0.06
American Robin	*Turdus migratorius*	0.03
Anhinga	*Anhinga anhinga*	0.03
Bald Eagle	*Haliaeetus leucocephalus*	0.03
Blackpoll Warbler	*Dendroica striata*	0.03
Eastern Kingbird	*Tyrannus tyrannus*	0.03
Great Egret	*Ardea alba*	0.03
Least Flycatcher	*Empidonax minimus*	0.03
Louisiana Waterthrush	*Seiurus motacilla*	0.03
Mississippi Kite	*Ictinia mississippiensis*	0.03
Orchard Oriole	*Icterus spurius*	0.03
Red-breasted Nuthatch	*Sitta canadensis*	0.03
Red-winged Blackbird	*Agelaius phoeniceus*	0.03
Solitary Sandpiper	*Tringa solitaria*	0.03
Wood Thrush	*Hylocichla mustelina*	0.03
Yellow-breasted Chat	*Icteria virens*	0.03

New Species Records

One new bird species was added to the CONG species list as a result of the 2009 monitoring efforts (Table 3): barred owl.

Table 3. New bird species detected at Congaree National Park and recommended NPSpecies classifications.

Common Name(s)	Abundance	Residency	Nativity	Pest	Management Priority	Exploitation Concerns
Barred Owl	Rare	Breeder	Native	No	No	No

Distribution
No species were detected in all sampling locations; however, Carolina wren and Northern cardinal were detected in 97% of the sampling locations. Northern parula and tufted titmouse were detected in 94% of the sampling locations, and blue-gray gnatcatcher, Acadian flycatcher, red-bellied woodpecker, red-eyed vireo, and yellow-billed cuckoo were detected in approximately 80% of the locations (Appendix D).

Appendix D contains distribution maps for all species detected during surveys. The sampling locations where each species was detected and was not detected are depicted on each map.

Diversity
Diversity indices calculated for these data were selected to reflect community composition (i.e., number of species) and structure (i.e., number of individuals), which include species richness and evenness estimates (Table 4). Confidence intervals for each diversity index were estimated with a bootstrap procedure. A brief explanation of interpreting the value is presented in Table 1.

Rank-abundance plots, frequency distributions, and other descriptive approaches were used to explore the abundance distributions and patterns in the dataset, and evaluate the utility of select indices and abundance equitability among species. The data are best fit by a log-normal abundance model; $\chi^2=4.6381$, df=5, p=0.5910. The dispersion (i.e., the variance / mean) also suggest that species are not aggregated and occur uniformly across the Park.

The species accumulation curve generated from the data asymptotes at approximately 28 samples (i.e., less than the total number of samples collected), validating the sample size as effective in characterizing bird diversity at the Park.

Observed species richness (i.e., S_{obs}) was 68 (95% CI: 60.57, 75.42). Most species-richness estimators are relatively consistent with one another, ranging from 74.70 – 91.15 (Table 4). Diversity indices suggest high bird-species diversity at the Park ($\alpha=16.26$, Q=17.07; Table 4). The sample was relatively well distributed among species, with four species only composing approximately 30% of the sample (Figure 3). The consistent performance of the evenness/dominance indices (i.e., E_{var}, $E_{1/D}$, E_g, and D_{BP}) suggest varied relative abundances of the species in the sample and a compositionally diverse bird community at the Park (Figure 3). Because 2009 monitoring efforts were the first for this vital sign at the Park, these values will serve as a baseline for comparison with future monitoring efforts.

Table 4. Bird alpha-diversity estimates at Congaree National Park, 2009.

Index	Symbol	Value	Lower 95% CI	Upper 95% CI	Value Interpretation
Native Spp. Richness	S_{obs}	68.00	60.57	75.42	Number of native species detected
Chao 1	**Chao1**	81.00	71.55	115.56	Estimated true species richness
Chao 2	**Chao2**	82.53	72.27	117.43	Estimated true species richness
Abundance-based Coverage	**ACE**	77.12	72.89	81.35	Estimated true species richness
Incidence-based Coverage	**ICE**	78.63	73.63	83.63	Estimated true species richness
Jackknife 1	**Jack1**	82.53	73.10	91.96	Estimated true species richness
Jackknife 2	**Jack2**	91.15	82.58	99.72	Estimated true species richness
Bootstrap	**Boot**	74.70	72.45	76.95	Estimated true species richness
Fisher's α	α	16.26	14.24	18.28	Baseline value, suggests high diversity
Q Statistic	**Q**	17.07	12.97	18.40	Baseline value, suggests high diversity
Smith and Wilson	E_{var}	0.32	0.30	0.38	Species occur in several relative abundances –low evenness
Smith and Wilson 1/D	$E_{1/D}$	0.34	0.33	0.39	Species occur in several relative abundances –low evenness
Camargo	**E'**				Invalid calculation due to dataset (i.e., too many locations with few detections)
Gini	E_G	0.36	0.29	0.43	Species occur in several relative abundances –low evenness
Berger-Parker	D_{BP}	0.10	0.08	0.11	Sample is not dominated by a single species, diverse assemblage of species

Literature Cited

Begon, M., J. L. Harper, and C. R. Townsend. 1986. Ecology: Individuals, populations and communities. Blackwell Scientific, Oxford, UK.

Berger, W. H., and F. L. Parker. 1970. Diversity of planktonic foraminifera in deep-sea sediments. Science 168:1345-1347.

Boyle, T. P., J. Sebaugh, and E. Robinson-Wilson. 1984. A hierarchical approach to the measurement of changes in community structure induced by environmental stress. Journal of Testing and Evaluation 12:241-245.

Bradford, D. F., S. E. Franson, A. C. Neale, D. T. Heggem, G. R. Miller, and G. E. Canterbury. 1998. Bird species assemblages as indicators of biological integrity in Great Basin rangeland. Environmental Monitoring and Assessment 49:1–22.

Bryce, S. A., R. M. Hughes, and P. R. Kaufmann. 2002. Development of a bird integrity index: Using bird assemblages as indicators of riparian condition. Environmental Management 30:294-310.

Buckland, S. T., D. R. Anderson, K. P. Burnham, and J. L. Laake. 1993. Distance Sampling: Estimating Abundance of Biological Populations. Chapman and Hall, New York.

Buckland, S. T., D. R. Anderson, K. P. Burnham, J. L. Laake, D. L. Borchers, and L. Thomas. 2001. Introduction to distance sampling: Estimating abundance of biological populations. Oxford University Press. 432 pp.

Burnham, K. P., and W. S. Overton. 1978. Estimation of the size of a closed population when capture probabilities vary among animals. Biometrika 65:623-633.

Burnham, K. P., and W. S. Overton. 1979. Robust estimation of population size when capture probabilities vary among animals. Ecology 60:927-936.

Butler, C. J. 2003. The disproportionate effect of global warming on the arrival dates of short-distant migratory birds in North America. Ibis 145:484-495.

Byrne, M. W. 2009. Sampling-point generation for SECN monitoring protocols: Generating a spatially-balanced random sample with the RRQRR tool in ArcGIS 9.1. Draft Standard Operating Procedure Version 1.0, last updated March 2009.

Byrne, M. W., B. D. Smrekar, C. J. Wright, and E. Thompson. *In preparation*. Draft bird community monitoring in Southeast Coast Network parks. USDI National Park Service, Southeast Coast Network, Atlanta, GA, USA.

Camargo, J. A. 1992. New diversity index for assessing structural alterations in aquatic communities. Bulletin of Environmental Contamination and Toxicology 48:428-434.

Chao, A. 1984. Non-parametric estimation of the number of classes in a population. Scandinavian Journal of Statistics 11:265-270.

Chao, A. 1987. Estimating the population size for capture-recapture data with unequal catchability. Biometrics 43:783-791.

Chao, A., and S. M Lee. 1992. Estimating the number of classes via sample coverage. Journal of the American Statistical Association 87:210-217.

Chazdon, R. L., R. K. Colwell, J. S. Denslow, and M. R. Guariguata. 1998. Statistical methods for estimating species richness of woody regeneration in primary and secondary rain forests of NE Costa Rica. Pp. 285-309 in F. Dallmeier and J. A. Comiskey, eds., Forest biodiversity research, monitoring and modeling: Conceptual background and Old World case studies. Parthenon Publishing, Paris, FR.

Colwell, R. K., and D. C. Lees. 2000. The mid-domain effect: Geometric constraints on the geography of species richness. Trends in Ecology and Evolution 15:70–76.

Coppedge, B. R., D. M. Engle, R. E. Masters, and M.S. Gregory. 2006. Development of a grassland index based on breeding bird assemblages. Environmental Monitoring and Assessment 118:125–145.

Croonquist, M. J., and R. P. Brooks. 1991. Use of avian and mammalian guilds as indicators of cumulative impacts in riparian-wetland areas. Environmental Management 15:701-714.

DeVivo, J. C., C. J. Wright, M. W. Byrne, E. DiDonato, and T. Curtis. 2008. Vital signs monitoring in the Southeast Coast Inventory & Monitoring Network. Natural Resource Report NPS/SECN/NRR—2008/061. National Park Service, Fort Collins, CO, USA.

Fancy, S. G. 1997. A new approach for analyzing bird densities from variable circular-plot counts. Pacific Science 51:107-114.

Fisher, R. A., A. S. Corbet, and C. B. Williams. 1943. The relation between the number of species and the number of individuals in a random sample of animal population. Journal of Animal Ecology 12:42–58.

Gini, C. 1912. Measurement of inequality on income. Economic Journal 31:22-43.

Haedrick, R. 1975. Diversity and overlap as measures of environmental quality. Water Research 9:945–949.

Hayek, L. A., and M. A. Buzas. 1997. Surveying natural populations. Columbia University Press, New York, USA.

Heltshe, J., and N. E. Forrester. 1983. Estimating species richness using the jackknife procedure. Biometrics 39:1-11.

Karr, J. R. 1991. Biological integrity: a long-neglected aspect of water resource management. Ecological Applications 1:66–84.

Karr, J. R., and E. W. Chu. 1995. Ecological integrity: Reclaiming lost connections. Pp. 34-48 *in* Westra, L., and J. Lemons (eds.), Perspective on ecological integrity. Kluwer Academic Publishing, NL.

Kempton, R. A., and L. R. Taylor. 1974. Log-series and log-normal parameters as diversity discriminants for the Lepidoptera. Journal of Animal Ecology 43:381–399.

Kempton, R. A., and L. R. Taylor. 1976. Models and statistics for species diversity. Nature 262:818–820.

Kempton, R. A., and L. R. Taylor. 1978. The Q-statistic and the diversity of floras. Nature 275:252-253.

Kempton, R. A., and R. W. M. Wedderburn. 1978. A comparison of three measures of species diversity. Biometrics 34:22-37.

Kempton, R. A. 2002. Species diversity. Encyclopedia of Environmetrics 4:2086-2092.

Lee, S. M., and A. Chao. 1994. Estimating population size via sample coverage for closed capture-recapture models. Biometrics 50:88-97.

Lexerød, N. L., and T. Eid. 2006. An evaluation of different diameter diversity indices based on criteria related to forest management planning. Forest Ecology and Management 222:17–28.

Lloyd, M., and R. J. Ghelardi. 1964. A table for calculating the "equitability" component of species diversity. Journal of Animal Ecology 33:217-225.

MacKenzie, D. I., J. D. Nichols, G. B. Lachman, S. Droege, J. A. Royle, and C. A. Langtimm. 2002. Estimating site occupancy when detection probabilities are less than one. Ecology 83:2248–2255.

Magurran, A. E. 1988. Ecological diversity and its measurement. Cambridge University Press, Cambridge, UK.

Magurran, A. E. 2004. Measuring biological diversity. Blackwell Publishing, Oxford, UK.

Margalef, D. R. 1958. Information theory in ecology. General Systems 3:36-71.

Marra, P. P., C. M. Francis, R. S. Mulvihill, and F .R. Moore. 2005. The influence of climate on the timing and rate of spring bird migration. Oecologia 142:307-315.

Maurer, B. A., and S. G. Heywood. 1993. Geographic range fragmentation and abundance in neotropical migratory birds. Conservation Biology 7:501-509.

McIntosh, R. I. 1967. An index of diversity and the relation of certain concepts to diversity. Ecology 48:392–404.

McNaughton, S. J. 1977. Diversity and stability of ecological communities: a comment on the role of empiricism in ecology. American Naturalist 111:515–525.

Montoya, J. M., and D. Raffaelli. 2010. Climate change, biotic interactions and ecosystem services. Philosophical Transactions of the Royal Society B 365: 2013–2018.

Mills A. M. 2005. Changes in the timing of spring and autumn migration in North American migrant passerines during a period of global warming. Ibis 147:259-260.

Murphy-Klassen H. M., T. J. Underwood, S. G. Sealy, and A. A. Czyrnyj. 2005. Long-term trends in spring arrival dates of migrant birds at Delta Marsh, Manitoba in relation to climate change. Auk 122:1130-1148.

Niven, D. K., G. S. Butcher, and G. T. Bancroft. 2009. Christmas bird counts and climate change: Northward shifts in early winter abundance. American Birds 82:10-15. Available online: http://web4.audubon.org/bird/cbc/pdf/AB_109_CBC_and_Climate_Change.pdf.

NPSpecies - The National Park Service Biodiversity Database. Secure online version. https://science1.nature.nps.gov/npspecies/web/main/start (Park list: accessed 1/13/2011).

O'Connell, T. L., L. E. Jackson, and R. P. Brooks. 2000. Bird guilds as indicators of ecological condition in the central Appalachians. Ecological Application 10:1706–1721.

Pielou, E. C. 1966. Species-diversity and pattern-diversity in the study of ecological succession. Journal of Theoretical Biology 10:370-383.

Ralph, C. J., G. R. Geupel, P. Pyle, T. E. Martin, and D. F. DeSante. 1993. Handbook of field methods for monitoring birds. General technical Report PSW-GTR-144-www. USDI Forest Service, Pacific Southwest Research Station, Albany, CA. 41 pp.

Reynolds , R. T., J. M. Scott, and R. A. Nussbaum. 1980. A variable circular-plot method for estimating bird numbers. Condor 82:309-313.

Sauer J. R., J. E. Hines, G. Hough, I. Thomas, and B. G. Peterjohn. 1997. The North American Breeding bird Survey Results and Analysis. Version 96.4. Patuxent Wildlife Research Center. Laurel, Maryland.

Simpson, E. H. 1949. Measurement of diversity. Nature 163:688.

Smith, B., and J. B. Wilson. 1996. A consumer's guide to evenness measures. Oikos 76:70-82.

Smith, E. P. and G. van Belle. 1984. Nonparametric estimation of species richness. Biometrics 40:119-129.

Strode, P. K. 2003. Implications of climate change for North American wood warblers (Parulidae). Global Change Biology 9:1137-1144.

Theobald, D. M., D. L. Stevens, D. White, N. S. Urquhart, A. R. Olsen, and J. B. Norman. 2007. Using GIS to generate spatially balanced random survey designs for natural resource applications. Environmental Management 40:134-146.

United States Geological Survey. 2011. (DRAFT) DOI Southeast Climate Science Center Operational and Science Plan. U.S. Geological Survey Open-File Report. 2011-0000 (publication pending).

Visser, M. E., and C. Both. 2005. Shifts in phenology due to global climate change: The need for a yardstick. Proceedings of the Royal Society 272:2561-2569.

Watson, C., and K. Malloy. 2006. The South Atlantic migratory bird initiative implementation plan: An integrated approach to conservation of all birds across all habitats, version 3.1. Atlantic Coast Joint Venture. Available online: http://www.acjv.org/documents/SAMBI_Plan3.2.pdf.

Whittaker, R. H. 1972. Evolution and measurement of species diversity. Taxon 21:213-251.

Wolda, H. 1983. Diversity, diversity indices and tropical cockroaches. Oecologia 58:290–298.

Wright, C. J., E. Thompson, B. A. Blankley, M. W. Byrne, T. Curtis, and M. B. Gregory. 2011. Summary of weather and climate monitoring in Southeast Coast Network parks, 2010. Natural Resource Data Series NPS/SECN/NRDS—2011/XXX. National Park Service, Fort Collins, Colorado.

Appendix A. Birds known to occur at CONG.

Table A-1. Birds known to occur at CONG based upon records in NPSpecies (2011) and those detected during this sampling effort.

Order	Family	Scientific Name	Common Name	NPSpecies	VCP 2009
Anseriformes	Anatidae	*Aix sponsa*	Wood Duck	X	
Anseriformes	Anatidae	*Anas americana*	American Wigeon	X	
Anseriformes	Anatidae	*Anas clypeata*	Northern Shoveler	X	
Anseriformes	Anatidae	*Anas crecca*	Green-winged Teal	X	
Anseriformes	Anatidae	*Anas discors*	Blue-winged Teal	X	
Anseriformes	Anatidae	*Anas platyrhynchos*	Mallard	X	
Anseriformes	Anatidae	*Anas rubripes*	American Black Duck	X	
Anseriformes	Anatidae	*Aythya collaris*	Ring-necked Duck	X	
Anseriformes	Anatidae	*Branta canadensis*	Canada Goose	X	
Anseriformes	Anatidae	*Lophodytes cucullatus*	Hooded Merganser	X	
Galliformes	Odontophoridae	*Colinus virginianus*	Northern Bobwhite	X	
Galliformes	Phasianidae	*Meleagris gallopavo*	Wild Turkey	X	X
Podicipediformes	Podicipedidae	*Podilymbus podiceps*	Pied-billed Grebe	X	
Ciconiiformes	Ciconiidae	*Mycteria americana*	Wood Stork	X	
Suliformes	Phalacrocoracidae	*Phalacrocorax auritus*	Double-crested Cormorant	X	
Suliformes	Anhingidae	*Anhinga anhinga*	Anhinga	X	X
Pelecaniformes	Ardeidae	*Ardea alba*	Great Egret	X	X
Pelecaniformes	Ardeidae	*Ardea herodias*	Great Blue Heron	X	X
Pelecaniformes	Ardeidae	*Botaurus lentiginosus*	American Bittern	X	
Pelecaniformes	Ardeidae	*Bubulcus ibis*	Cattle Egret	X	
Pelecaniformes	Ardeidae	*Butorides virescens*	Green Heron	X	
Pelecaniformes	Ardeidae	*Egretta caerulea*	Little Blue Heron	X	
Pelecaniformes	Ardeidae	*Egretta thula*	Snowy Egret	X	
Pelecaniformes	Ardeidae	*Nyctanassa violacea*	Yellow-crowned Night-Heron	X	
Pelecaniformes	Threskiornithidae	*Ajaia ajaja*	Roseate Spoonbill	X	
Pelecaniformes	Threskiornithidae	*Eudocimus albus*	White Ibis	X	
Accipitriformes	Cathartidae	*Cathartes aura*	Turkey Vulture	X	X
Accipitriformes	Cathartidae	*Coragyps atratus*	Black Vulture	X	
Accipitriformes	Pandionidae	*Pandion haliaetus*	Osprey	X	
Accipitriformes	Accipitridae	*Accipiter cooperii*	Cooper's Hawk	X	
Accipitriformes	Accipitridae	*Accipiter striatus*	Sharp-shinned Hawk	X	
Accipitriformes	Accipitridae	*Aquila chrysaetos*	Golden Eagle	X	
Accipitriformes	Accipitridae	*Buteo jamaicensis*	Red-tailed Hawk	X	X
Accipitriformes	Accipitridae	*Buteo lineatus*	Red-shouldered Hawk	X	X
Accipitriformes	Accipitridae	*Buteo platypterus*	Broad-winged Hawk	X	
Accipitriformes	Accipitridae	*Buteo swainsoni*	Swainson's Hawk	X	
Accipitriformes	Accipitridae	*Circus cyaneus*	Northern Harrier	X	
Accipitriformes	Accipitridae	*Elanoides forficatus*	Swallow-tailed Kite	X	
Accipitriformes	Accipitridae	*Haliaeetus leucocephalus*	Bald Eagle	X	X
Accipitriformes	Accipitridae	*Ictinia mississippiensis*	Mississippi Kite	X	X
Falconiformes	Falconidae	*Falco columbarius*	Merlin	X	

Table A-1. Continued.

Order	Family	Scientific Name	Common Name	NPSpecies	VCP 2009
Falconiformes	Falconidae	*Falco peregrinus*	Peregrine Falcon	X	
Falconiformes	Falconidae	*Falco sparverius*	American Kestrel	X	
Charadriiformes	Charadriidae	*Charadrius vociferus*	Killdeer	X	
Charadriiformes	Scolopacidae	*Actitis macularia*	Spotted Sandpiper	X	
Charadriiformes	Scolopacidae	*Gallinago gallinago*	Common Snipe	X	
Charadriiformes	Scolopacidae	*Scolopax minor*	American Woodcock	X	
Charadriiformes	Scolopacidae	*Tringa flavipes*	Lesser Yellowlegs	X	
Charadriiformes	Scolopacidae	*Tringa solitaria*	Solitary Sandpiper	X	X
Charadriiformes	Laridae	*Larus delawarensis*	Ring-billed Gull	X	
Charadriiformes	Laridae	*Larus philadelphia*	Bonaparte's Gull	X	
Charadriiformes	Laridae	*Sterna caspia*	Caspian Tern	X	
Charadriiformes	Alcidae	*Uria lomvia*	Thick-billed Murre	X	
Columbiformes	Columbidae	*Columba livia*	Rock Pigeon	X	
Columbiformes	Columbidae	*Streptopelia decaocto*	Eurasian Collared-Dove	X	
Columbiformes	Columbidae	*Zenaida macroura*	Mourning Dove	X	X
Cuculiformes	Cuculidae	*Coccyzus americanus*	Yellow-billed Cuckoo	X	X
Cuculiformes	Cuculidae	*Coccyzus erythropthalmus*	Black-billed Cuckoo	X	
Strigiformes	Strigidae	*Bubo virginianus*	Great Horned Owl	X	
Strigiformes	Strigidae	*Megascops asio*	Eastern Screech-Owl	X	
Strigiformes	Strigidae	*Strix varia*	Barred Owl		X
Caprimulgiformes	Caprimulgidae	*Caprimulgus carolinensis*	Chuck-will's-widow	X	
Caprimulgiformes	Caprimulgidae	*Caprimulgus vociferus*	Eastern Whip-poor-will	X	
Caprimulgiformes	Caprimulgidae	*Chordeiles minor*	Common Nighthawk	X	
Apodiformes	Apodidae	*Chaetura pelagica*	Chimney Swift	X	X
Apodiformes	Trochilidae	*Archilochus colubris*	Ruby-throated Hummingbird	X	X
Coraciiformes	Alcedinidae	*Megaceryle alcyon*	Belted Kingfisher	X	X
Piciformes	Picidae	*Colaptes auratus*	Northern Flicker	X	
Piciformes	Picidae	*Dryocopus pileatus*	Pileated Woodpecker	X	X
Piciformes	Picidae	*Melanerpes carolinus*	Red-bellied Woodpecker	X	X
Piciformes	Picidae	*Melanerpes erythrocephalus*	Red-headed Woodpecker	X	X
Piciformes	Picidae	*Picoides pubescens*	Downy Woodpecker	X	X
Piciformes	Picidae	*Picoides villosus*	Hairy Woodpecker	X	X
Piciformes	Picidae	*Sphyrapicus varius*	Yellow-bellied Sapsucker	X	
Passeriformes	Tyrannidae	*Contopus cooperi*	Olive-sided Flycatcher	X	
Passeriformes	Tyrannidae	*Contopus virens*	Eastern Wood-Pewee	X	X
Passeriformes	Tyrannidae	*Empidonax minimus*	Least Flycatcher	X	X
Passeriformes	Tyrannidae	*Empidonax virescens*	Acadian Flycatcher	X	X
Passeriformes	Tyrannidae	*Myiarchus crinitus*	Great Crested Flycatcher	X	X
Passeriformes	Tyrannidae	*Sayornis phoebe*	Eastern Phoebe	X	
Passeriformes	Tyrannidae	*Tyrannus tyrannus*	Eastern Kingbird	X	X
Passeriformes	Tyrannidae	*Tyrannus verticalis*	Western Kingbird	X	

Table A-1. Continued.

Order	Family	Scientific Name	Common Name	NPSpecies	VCP 2009
Passeriformes	Laniidae	*Lanius ludovicianus*	Loggerhead Shrike	X	
Passeriformes	Vireonidae	*Vireo flavifrons*	Yellow-throated Vireo	X	X
Passeriformes	Vireonidae	*Vireo gilvus*	Warbling Vireo	X	
Passeriformes	Vireonidae	*Vireo griseus*	White-eyed Vireo	X	X
Passeriformes	Vireonidae	*Vireo olivaceus*	Red-eyed Vireo	X	X
Passeriformes	Vireonidae	*Vireo philadelphicus*	Philadelphia Vireo	X	
Passeriformes	Vireonidae	*Vireo solitarius*	Blue-headed Vireo	X	X
Passeriformes	Corvidae	*Corvus brachyrhynchos*	American Crow	X	X
Passeriformes	Corvidae	*Corvus ossifragus*	Fish Crow	X	X
Passeriformes	Corvidae	*Cyanocitta cristata*	Blue Jay	X	X
Passeriformes	Hirundinidae	*Hirundo rustica*	Barn Swallow	X	X
Passeriformes	Hirundinidae	*Petrochelidon pyrrhonota*	Cliff Swallow	X	
Passeriformes	Hirundinidae	*Progne subis*	Purple Martin	X	
Passeriformes	Hirundinidae	*Riparia riparia*	Bank Swallow	X	
Passeriformes	Hirundinidae	*Stelgidopteryx serripennis*	Northern Rough-winged Swallow	X	
Passeriformes	Hirundinidae	*Tachycineta bicolor*	Tree Swallow	X	
Passeriformes	Paridae	*Baeolophus bicolor*	Tufted Titmouse	X	X
Passeriformes	Paridae	*Poecile carolinensis*	Carolina Chickadee	X	X
Passeriformes	Sittidae	*Sitta canadensis*	Red-breasted Nuthatch	X	X
Passeriformes	Sittidae	*Sitta carolinensis*	White-breasted Nuthatch	X	X
Passeriformes	Sittidae	*Sitta pusilla*	Brown-headed Nuthatch	X	
Passeriformes	Certhiidae	*Certhia americana*	Brown Creeper	X	
Passeriformes	Troglodytidae	*Thryothorus ludovicianus*	Carolina Wren	X	X
Passeriformes	Troglodytidae	*Troglodytes aedon*	House Wren	X	
Passeriformes	Troglodytidae	*Troglodytes troglodytes*	Winter Wren	X	
Passeriformes	Polioptilidae	*Polioptila caerulea*	Blue-gray Gnatcatcher	X	X
Passeriformes	Regulidae	*Regulus calendula*	Ruby-crowned Kinglet	X	
Passeriformes	Regulidae	*Regulus satrapa*	Golden-crowned Kinglet	X	
Passeriformes	Turdidae	*Catharus bicknelli*	Bicknell's Thrush	X	
Passeriformes	Turdidae	*Catharus fuscescens*	Veery	X	
Passeriformes	Turdidae	*Catharus guttatus*	Hermit Thrush	X	
Passeriformes	Turdidae	*Catharus minimus*	Gray-cheeked Thrush	X	
Passeriformes	Turdidae	*Catharus ustulatus*	Swainson's Thrush	X	
Passeriformes	Turdidae	*Hylocichla mustelina*	Wood Thrush	X	X
Passeriformes	Turdidae	*Sialia sialis*	Eastern Bluebird	X	
Passeriformes	Turdidae	*Turdus migratorius*	American Robin	X	X
Passeriformes	Mimidae	*Dumetella carolinensis*	Gray Catbird	X	
Passeriformes	Mimidae	*Mimus polyglottos*	Northern Mockingbird	X	
Passeriformes	Mimidae	*Toxostoma rufum*	Brown Thrasher	X	
Passeriformes	Sturnidae	*Sturnus vulgaris*	European Starling	X	
Passeriformes	Motacillidae	*Anthus rubescens*	American Pipit	X	

Order	Family	Scientific Name	Common Name	NPSpecies	VCP 2009
Passeriformes	Bombycillidae	*Bombycilla cedrorum*	Cedar Waxwing	X	
Passeriformes	Parulidae	*Dendroica caerulescens*	Black-throated Blue Warbler	X	
Passeriformes	Parulidae	*Dendroica castanea*	Bay-breasted Warbler	X	
Passeriformes	Parulidae	*Dendroica cerulea*	Cerulean Warbler	X	
Passeriformes	Parulidae	*Dendroica coronata*	Yellow-rumped Warbler	X	
Passeriformes	Parulidae	*Dendroica discolor*	Prairie Warbler	X	X
Passeriformes	Parulidae	*Dendroica dominica*	Yellow-throated Warbler	X	X
Passeriformes	Parulidae	*Dendroica fusca*	Blackburnian Warbler	X	
Passeriformes	Parulidae	*Dendroica magnolia*	Magnolia Warbler	X	
Passeriformes	Parulidae	*Dendroica palmarum*	Palm Warbler	X	
Passeriformes	Parulidae	*Dendroica pensylvanica*	Chestnut-sided Warbler	X	
Passeriformes	Parulidae	*Dendroica petechia*	Yellow Warbler	X	
Passeriformes	Parulidae	*Dendroica pinus*	Pine Warbler	X	X
Passeriformes	Parulidae	*Dendroica striata*	Blackpoll Warbler	X	X
Passeriformes	Parulidae	*Dendroica tigrina*	Cape May Warbler	X	
Passeriformes	Parulidae	*Dendroica virens*	Black-throated Green Warbler	X	
Passeriformes	Parulidae	*Geothlypis trichas*	Common Yellowthroat	X	X
Passeriformes	Parulidae	*Helmitheros vermivorus*	Worm-eating Warbler	X	X
Passeriformes	Parulidae	*Icteria virens*	Yellow-breasted Chat	X	X
Passeriformes	Parulidae	*Limnothlypis swainsonii*	Swainson's Warbler	X	X
Passeriformes	Parulidae	*Mniotilta varia*	Black-and-white Warbler	X	X
Passeriformes	Parulidae	*Oporornis formosus*	Kentucky Warbler	X	X
Passeriformes	Parulidae	*Oporornis philadelphia*	Mourning Warbler	X	
Passeriformes	Parulidae	*Parula americana*	Northern Parula	X	X
Passeriformes	Parulidae	*Protonotaria citrea*	Prothonotary Warbler	X	X
Passeriformes	Parulidae	*Seiurus aurocapillus*	Ovenbird	X	X
Passeriformes	Parulidae	*Seiurus motacilla*	Louisiana Waterthrush	X	X
Passeriformes	Parulidae	*Seiurus noveboracensis*	Northern Waterthrush	X	
Passeriformes	Parulidae	*Setophaga ruticilla*	American Redstart	X	X
Passeriformes	Parulidae	*Vermivora celata*	Orange-crowned Warbler	X	
Passeriformes	Parulidae	*Vermivora chrysoptera*	Golden-winged Warbler	X	
Passeriformes	Parulidae	*Vermivora peregrina*	Tennessee Warbler	X	
Passeriformes	Parulidae	*Vermivora pinus*	Blue-winged Warbler	X	
Passeriformes	Parulidae	*Vermivora ruficapilla*	Nashville Warbler	X	
Passeriformes	Parulidae	*Wilsonia canadensis*	Canada Warbler	X	
Passeriformes	Parulidae	*Wilsonia citrina*	Hooded Warbler	X	X
Passeriformes	Emberizidae	*Aimophila aestivalis*	Bachman's Sparrow	X	
Passeriformes	Emberizidae	*Ammodramus henslowii*	Henslow's Sparrow	X	
Passeriformes	Emberizidae	*Junco hyemalis*	Dark-eyed Junco	X	
Passeriformes	Emberizidae	*Melospiza georgiana*	Swamp Sparrow	X	
Passeriformes	Emberizidae	*Melospiza lincolnii*	Lincoln's Sparrow	X	

Table A-1. Continued.

Order	Family	Scientific Name	Common Name	NPSpecies	VCP 2009
Passeriformes	Emberizidae	*Melospiza melodia*	Song Sparrow	X	X
Passeriformes	Emberizidae	*Passerculus sandwichensis*	Savannah Sparrow	X	
Passeriformes	Emberizidae	*Passerella iliaca*	Fox Sparrow	X	
Passeriformes	Emberizidae	*Pipilo erythrophthalmus*	Eastern Towhee	X	X
Passeriformes	Emberizidae	*Pooecetes gramineus*	Vesper Sparrow	X	
Passeriformes	Emberizidae	*Spizella passerina*	Chipping Sparrow	X	
Passeriformes	Emberizidae	*Spizella pusilla*	Field Sparrow	X	
Passeriformes	Emberizidae	*Zonotrichia albicollis*	White-throated Sparrow	X	
Passeriformes	Cardinalidae	*Cardinalis cardinalis*	Northern Cardinal	X	X
Passeriformes	Cardinalidae	*Guiraca caerulea*	Blue Grosbeak	X	X
Passeriformes	Cardinalidae	*Passerina cyanea*	Indigo Bunting	X	X
Passeriformes	Cardinalidae	*Pheucticus ludovicianus*	Rose-breasted Grosbeak	X	
Passeriformes	Cardinalidae	*Piranga olivacea*	Scarlet Tanager	X	
Passeriformes	Cardinalidae	*Piranga rubra*	Summer Tanager	X	X
Passeriformes	Icteridae	*Agelaius phoeniceus*	Red-winged Blackbird	X	X
Passeriformes	Icteridae	*Dolichonyx oryzivorus*	Bobolink	X	
Passeriformes	Icteridae	*Euphagus carolinus*	Rusty Blackbird	X	
Passeriformes	Icteridae	*Icterus galbula*	Baltimore Oriole	X	
Passeriformes	Icteridae	*Icterus spurius*	Orchard Oriole	X	X
Passeriformes	Icteridae	*Molothrus ater*	Brown-headed Cowbird	X	
Passeriformes	Icteridae	*Quiscalus quiscula*	Common Grackle	X	X
Passeriformes	Icteridae	*Sturnella magna*	Eastern Meadowlark	X	
Passeriformes	Fringillidae	*Carduelis pinus*	Pine Siskin	X	
Passeriformes	Fringillidae	*Carduelis tristis*	American Goldfinch	X	X
Passeriformes	Fringillidae	*Carpodacus mexicanus*	House Finch	X	
Passeriformes	Fringillidae	*Carpodacus purpureus*	Purple Finch	X	
Passeriformes	Fringillidae	*Coccothraustes vespertinus*	Evening Grosbeak	X	
Passeriformes	Passeridae	*Passer domesticus*	House Sparrow	X	

Appendix B. Map of sampling locations with point labels.

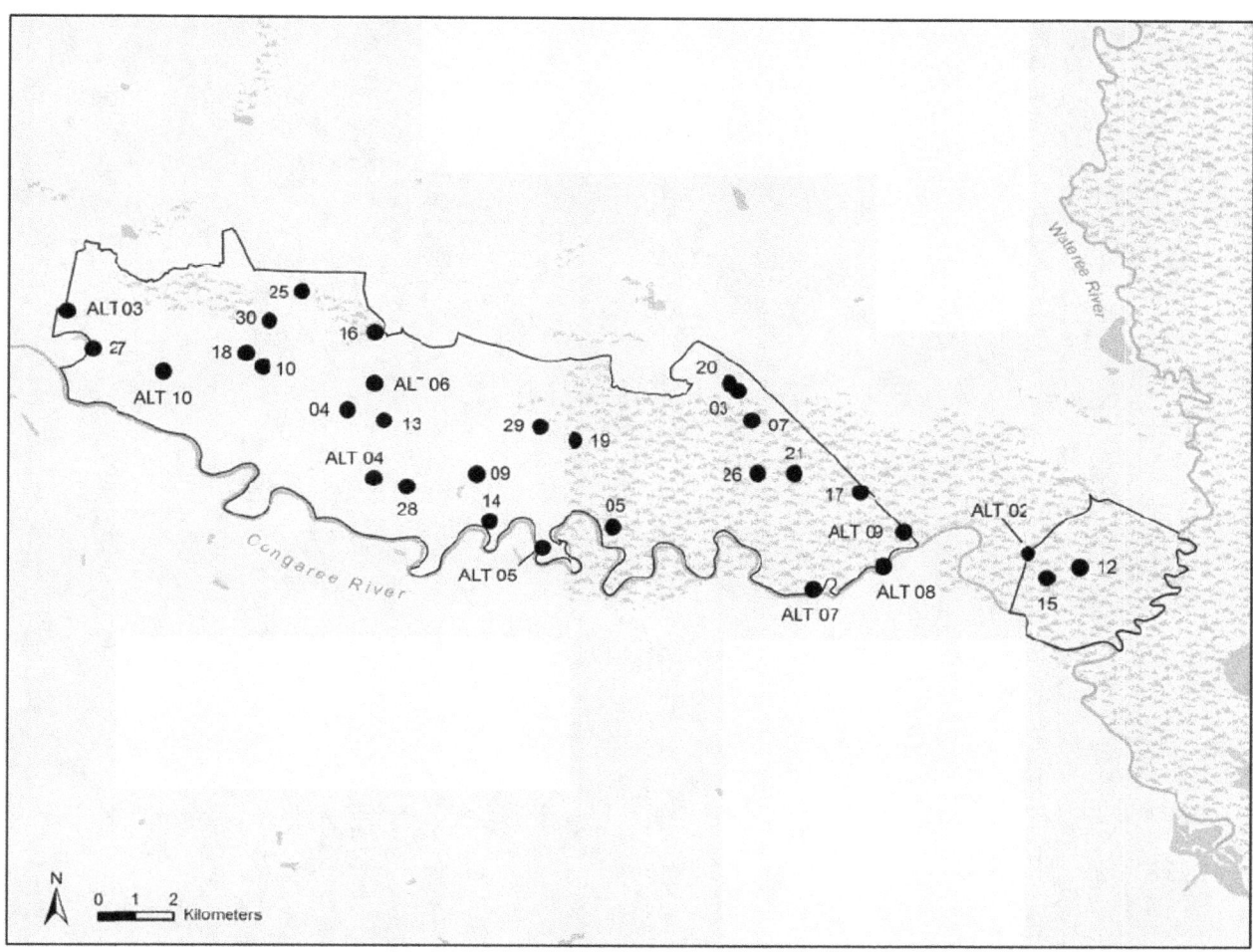

Figure B-1. Spatially- balanced random sampling locations at CONG with labels, 2009.

Appendix C. Species detections by sampling location.

Table C-1. Species detected at each sampling location at CONG, 2009. Refer to Appendix B for labeled sampling-locations.

Common Name	1	3	4	5	7	9	10	12	13	14	15	16	17	18	19	20	21	25	26	27	28	29	30	A2	A3	A4	A5	A6	A7	A8
Wild Turkey	X														X										X		X			X
Anhinga																											X			X
Great Blue Heron				X						X											X				X		X		X	X
Great Egret																														
Turkey Vulture								X																X						
Mississippi Kite																											X			
Bald Eagle	X																													
Red-shouldered Hawk							X	X			X			X	X	X		X		X	X		X		X	X		X	X	X
Red-tailed Hawk			X			X									X						X									X
Solitary Sandpiper	X																													
Mourning Dove					X											X														
Yellow-billed Cuckoo	X	X	X	X	X		X	X	X	X	X	X	X	X	X	X	X	X		X	X	X	X		X		X		X	X
Barred Owl		X	X				X		X	X				X	X	X	X	X		X				X				X		X
Chimney Swift				X																		X	X							
Ruby-throated Hummingbird								X														X		X						X
Belted Kingfisher	X			X																		X								
Red-headed Woodpecker				X															X											X
Red-bellied Woodpecker	X	X	X	X	X	X	X	X	X	X	X	X	X	X	X	X	X	X	X	X	X	X	X	X	X		X	X	X	X
Downy Woodpecker			X						X	X				X	X			X	X	X	X	X	X		X		X	X		X
Hairy Woodpecker																						X				X	X			
Pileated Woodpecker	X		X	X	X	X	X			X	X	X		X		X		X		X		X	X		X	X	X	X	X	X
Eastern Wood-Pewee									X			X				X		X			X	X	X		X	X			X	X
Acadian Flycatcher	X	X	X	X	X		X		X	X	X	X	X	X	X	X		X		X	X	X	X		X	X	X	X	X	X
Least Flycatcher						X																								
Great Crested Flycatcher				X			X	X						X				X		X					X		X			X
Eastern Kingbird																														
White-eyed Vireo	X	X	X	X	X		X	X	X	X	X	X				X		X	X	X	X			X	X		X	X	X	
Yellow-throated Vireo	X	X	X	X	X	X	X		X	X		X		X				X		X	X		X		X		X	X		
Blue-headed Vireo						X									X															
Red-eyed Vireo	X	X	X	X	X		X		X	X	X	X	X	X	X	X	X	X		X	X	X	X		X	X	X	X	X	X
Blue Jay								X								X		X				X	X							
American Crow	X	X	X	X	X		X	X		X	X	X	X			X	X	X	X			X			X					X

Table C-1. Continued.

Common Name	1	3	4	5	7	9	10	12	13	14	15	16	17	18	19	20	21	25	26	27	28	29	30	A2	A3	A4	A5	A6	A7	A8
																													Sampling Location	
Fish Crow																				X									X	
Barn Swallow																											X			
Carolina Chickadee		X	X	X		X		X	X		X	X		X	X	X	X	X	X	X	X		X	X	X		X	X	X	X
Tufted Titmouse	X	X	X	X	X		X	X	X	X	X	X	X	X	X	X	X	X	X	X	X	X	X	X	X	X	X	X	X	X
Red-breasted Nuthatch																		X												
White-breasted Nuthatch			X				X									X							X							
Carolina Wren	X	X	X	X	X	X	X	X	X	X	X	X	X	X	X	X	X	X	X	X	X	X	X	X	X	X	X	X	X	X
Blue-gray Gnatcatcher	X	X	X	X	X	X	X	X	X	X	X	X		X	X	X	X	X	X	X	X	X	X	X	X	X		X	X	X
Wood Thrush										X																				
American Robin																		X												
Ovenbird												X			X						X				X					
Worm-eating Warbler				X						X																X				
Louisiana Waterthrush																										X				
Black-and-white Warbler						X								X																
Prothonotary Warbler	X					X						X			X						X					X		X		X
Swainson's Warbler										X												X								
Kentucky Warbler				X															X		X					X				
Common Yellowthroat											X												X	X						
Hooded Warbler						X					X	X							X				X							
American Redstart	X							X									X			X										
Northern Parula	X	X			X	X	X	X	X	X	X	X		X	X	X	X	X	X	X	X		X	X	X	X	X	X	X	X
Blackpoll Warbler																										X				
Pine Warbler		X			X								X			X		X												
Yellow-throated Warbler			X							X	X	X			X						X						X	X		
Prairie Warbler						X														X			X							
Yellow-breasted Chat																												X		
Eastern Towhee		X																X						X	X					
Song Sparrow							X																	X						
Summer Tanager	X	X										X	X							X					X					
Northern Cardinal	X	X	X	X	X	X	X	X	X	X	X	X	X	X	X	X	X	X	X	X	X	X	X	X	X	X	X	X	X	X
Blue Grosbeak								X																X						
Indigo Bunting	X							X		X	X													X			X		X	X

41

Table C-1. Continued.

Common Name		Sampling Location																											
	1	3	4	5	7	9	10	12	13	14	15	16	17	18	19	20	21	25	26	27	28	29	30	A2	A3	A4	A5	A6	A7	A8
Red-winged Blackbird																													X	
Common Grackle											X													X			X	X		
Orchard Oriole																													X	
American Goldfinch					X			X					X																	

Appendix D. Distribution Maps

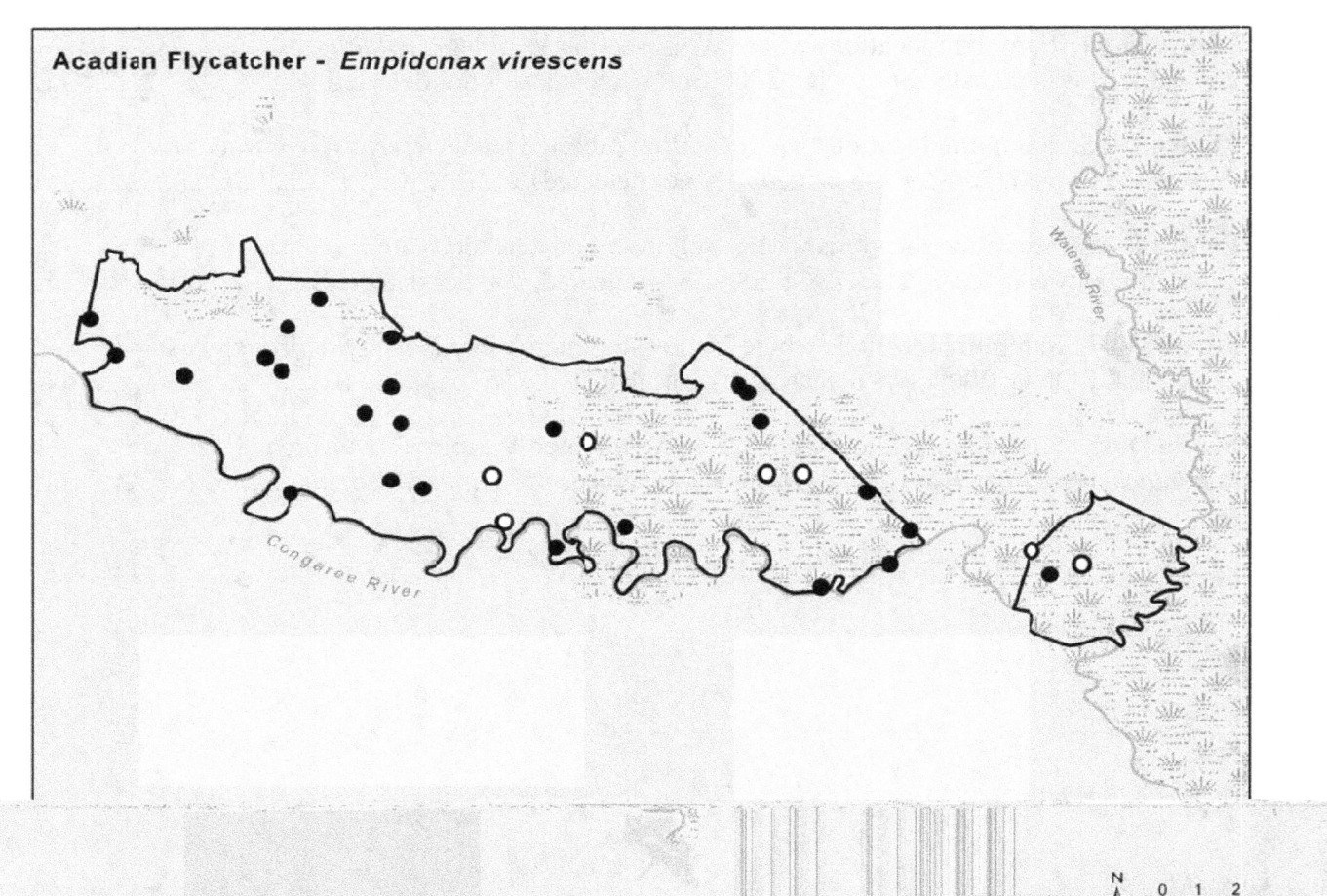

Acadian Flycatcher - *Empidonax virescens*

where Acadian Flycatcher (*Empidonax virescens*) was detected at
not detected.

Figure D·1. Sampling loca
CONG, 2009. ● = det cte

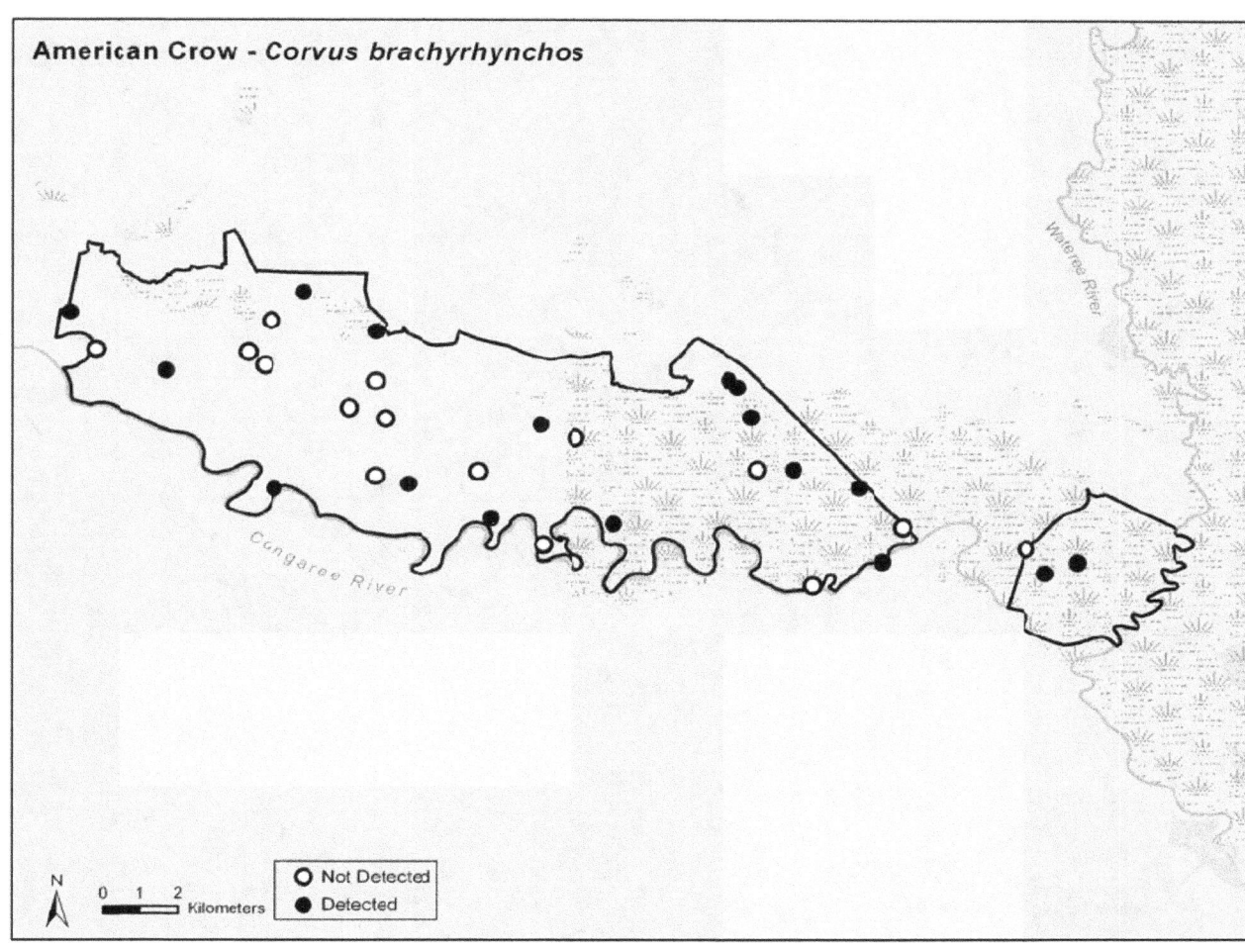

Figure D-2. Sampling locations where American Crow (*Corvus brachyrhynchos*) was detected at CONG, 2009. ● = detected, ○ = not detected.

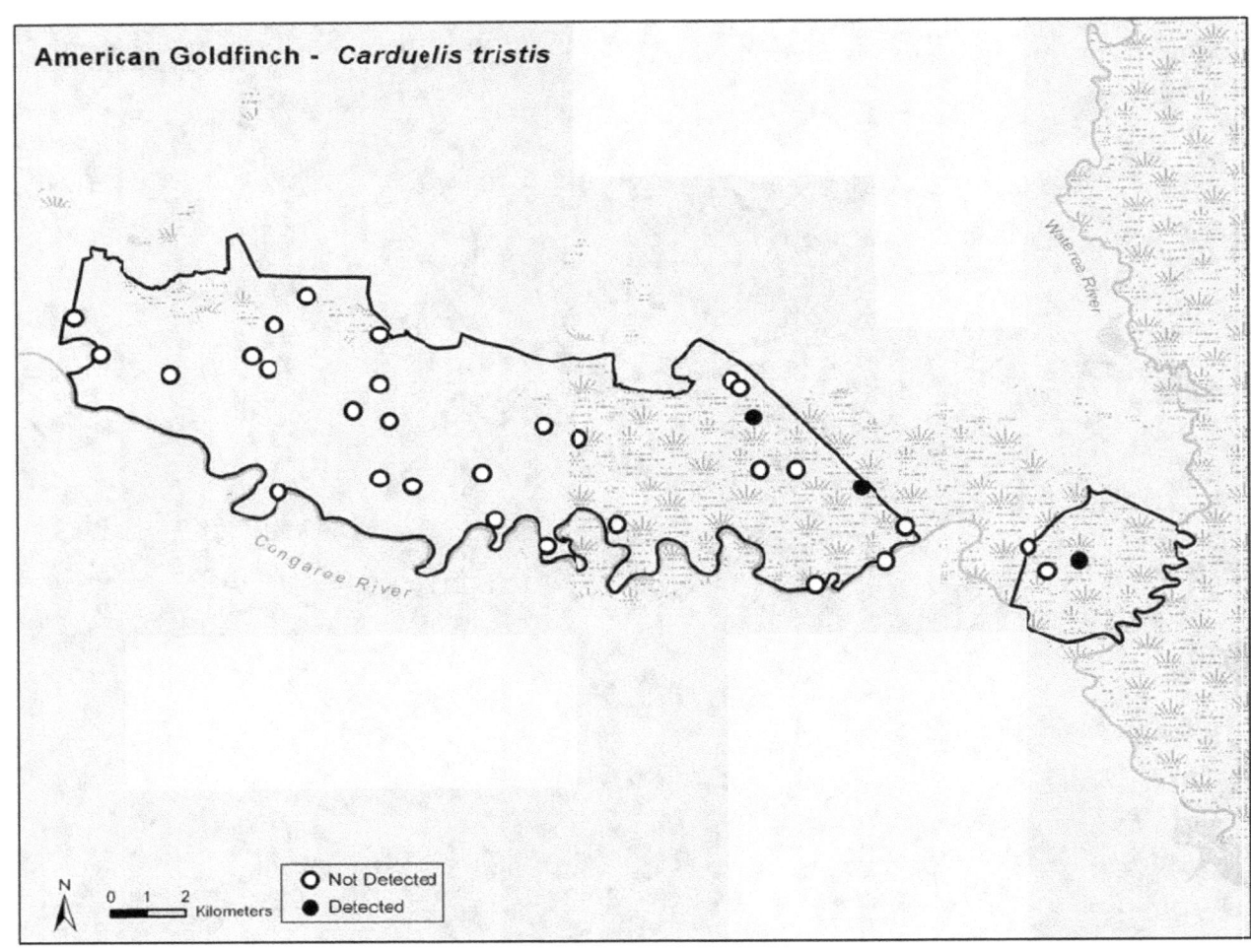

Figure D-3. Sampling locations where American Goldfinch (*Carduelis tristis*) was detected at CONG, 2009. ● = detected, ○ = not detected.

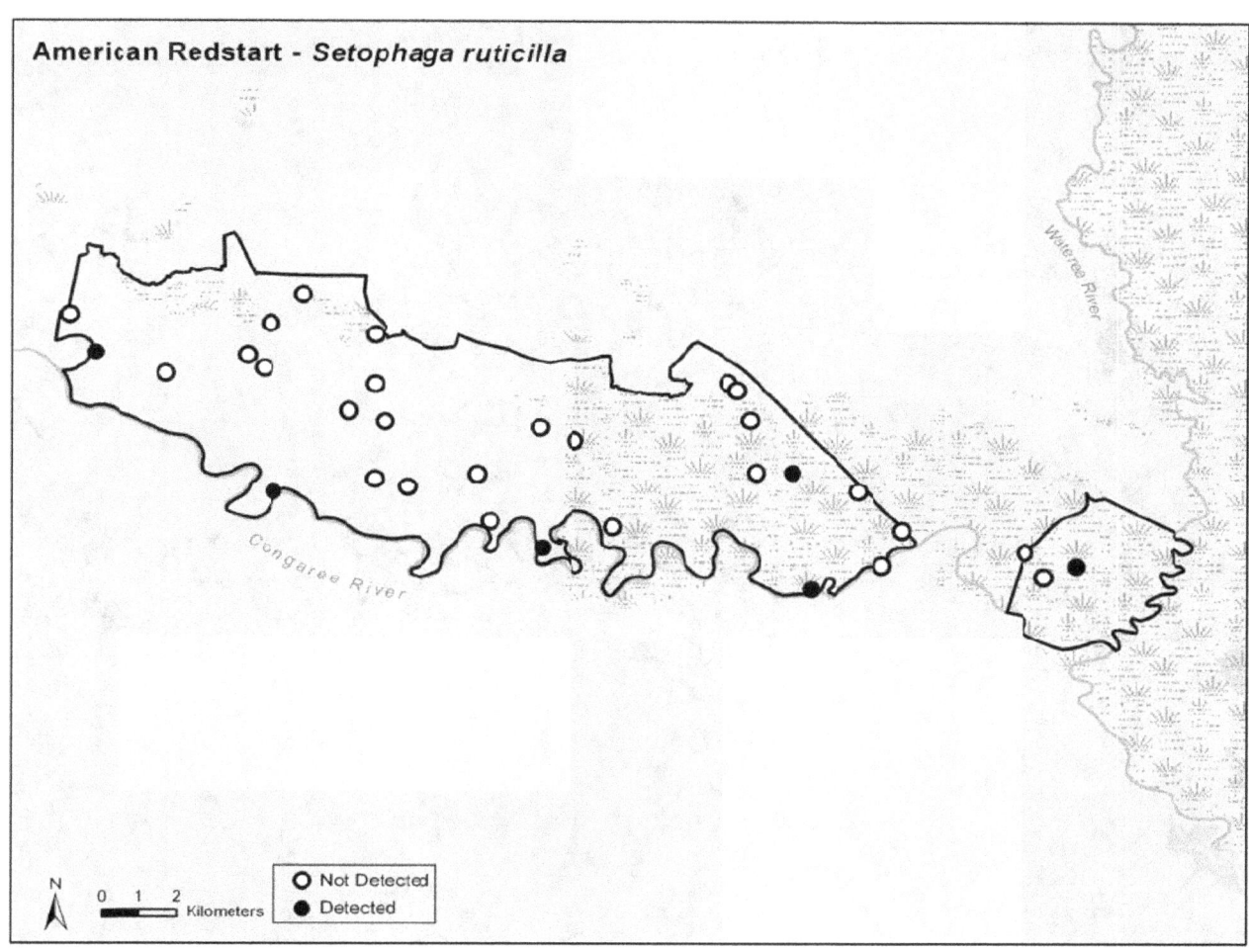

Figure D-4. Sampling locations where American Redstart (*Setophaga ruticilla*) was detected at CONG, 2009. • = detected, ○ = not detected.

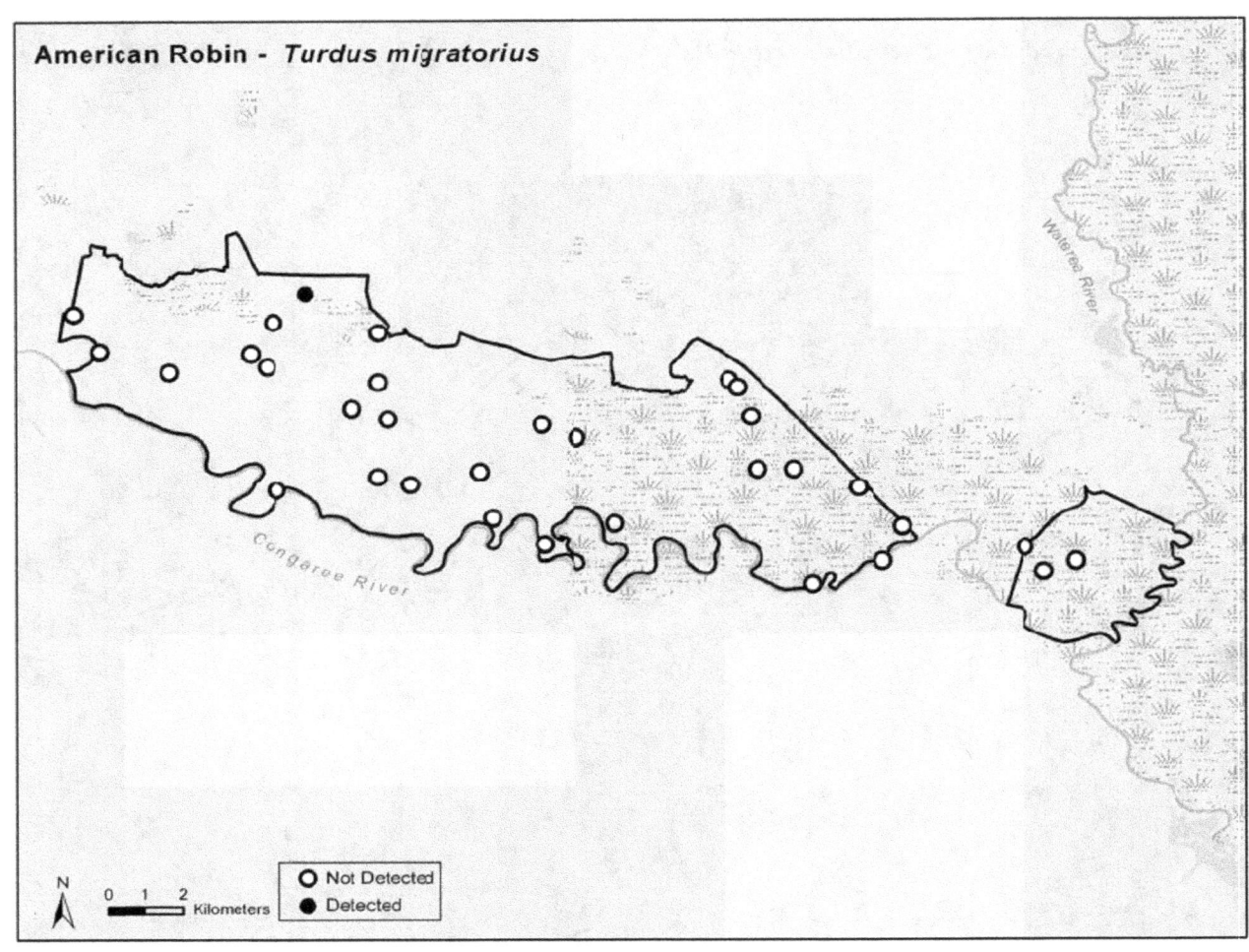

Figure D·5. Sampling locations where American Robin (*Tur lus migratori is*) was detected at CONG, 2009. ● = detected, ○ = not detected.

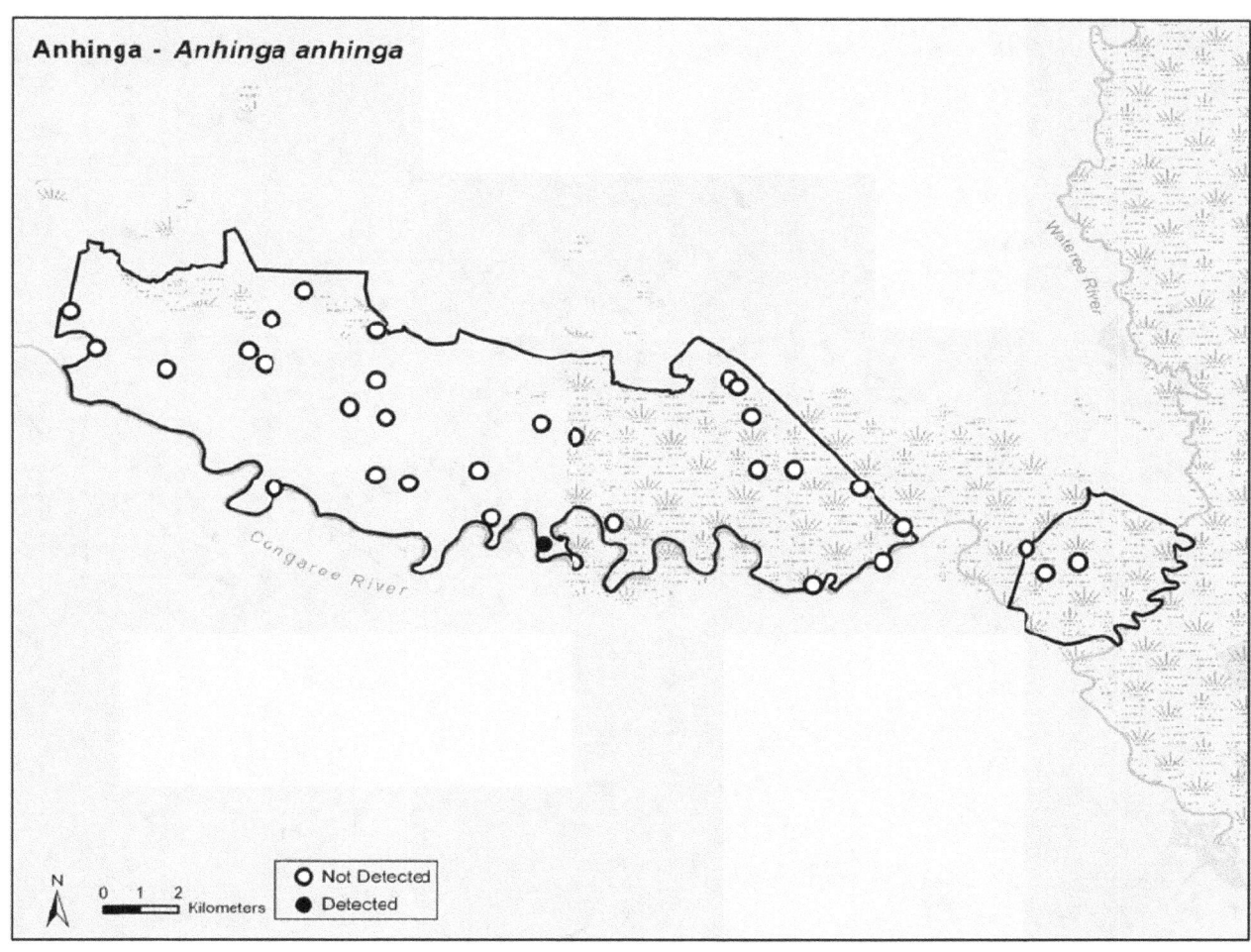

Figure D-6. Sampling locations where Anhinga (*Anhinga an⁊inga*) was d⁊tected at CONG, 2009. ● = detected, ○ = not detected.

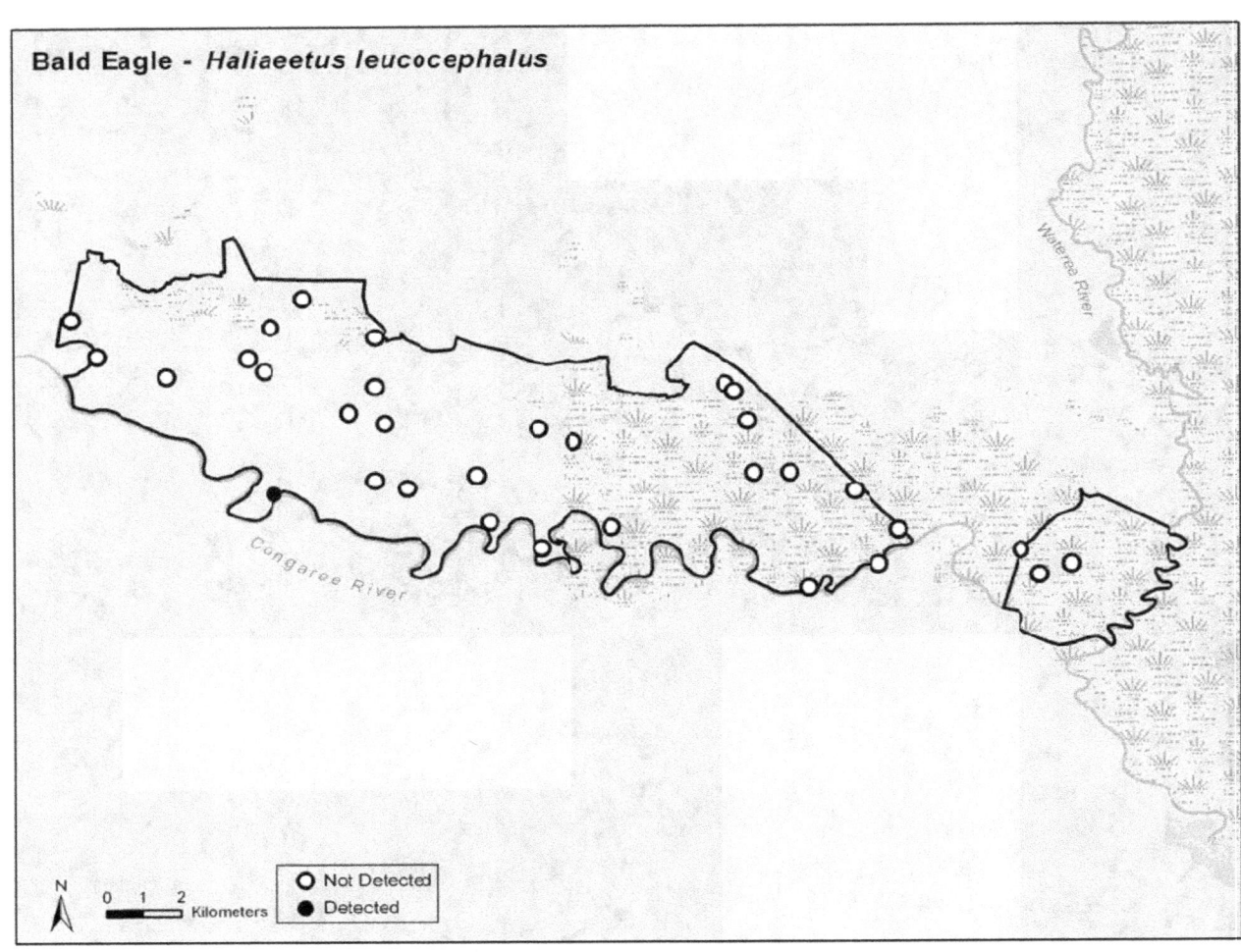

Figure D-7. Sampling locations where Bald Eagle (*Haliaeetus leucocephalus*) was detected at CONG, 2009. ● = detected, ○ = not detected.

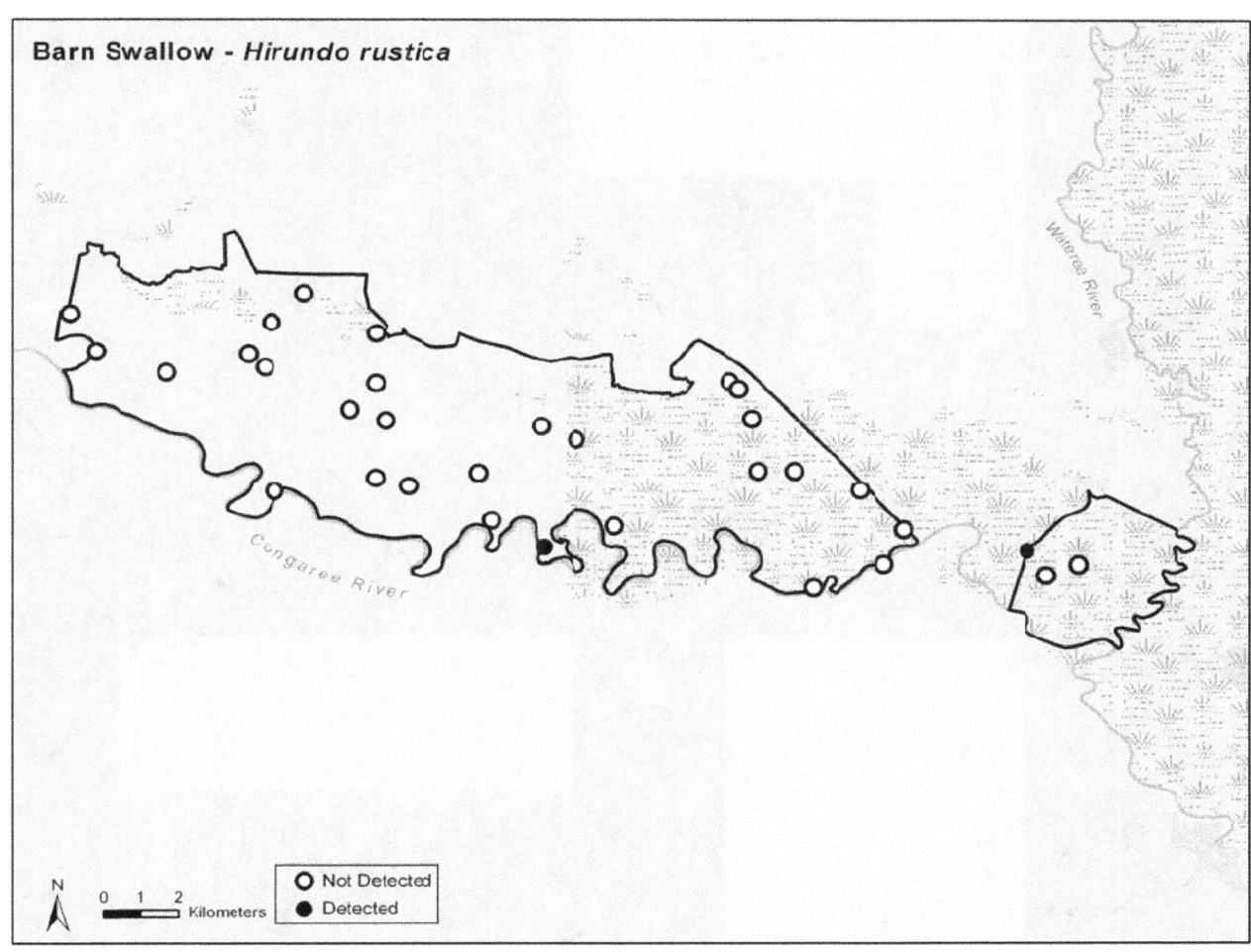

Figure D-8. Sampling locations where Barn Swallow (*Hirun o rustica*) was detected at CONG, 2009. • = detected, ○ = not detected.

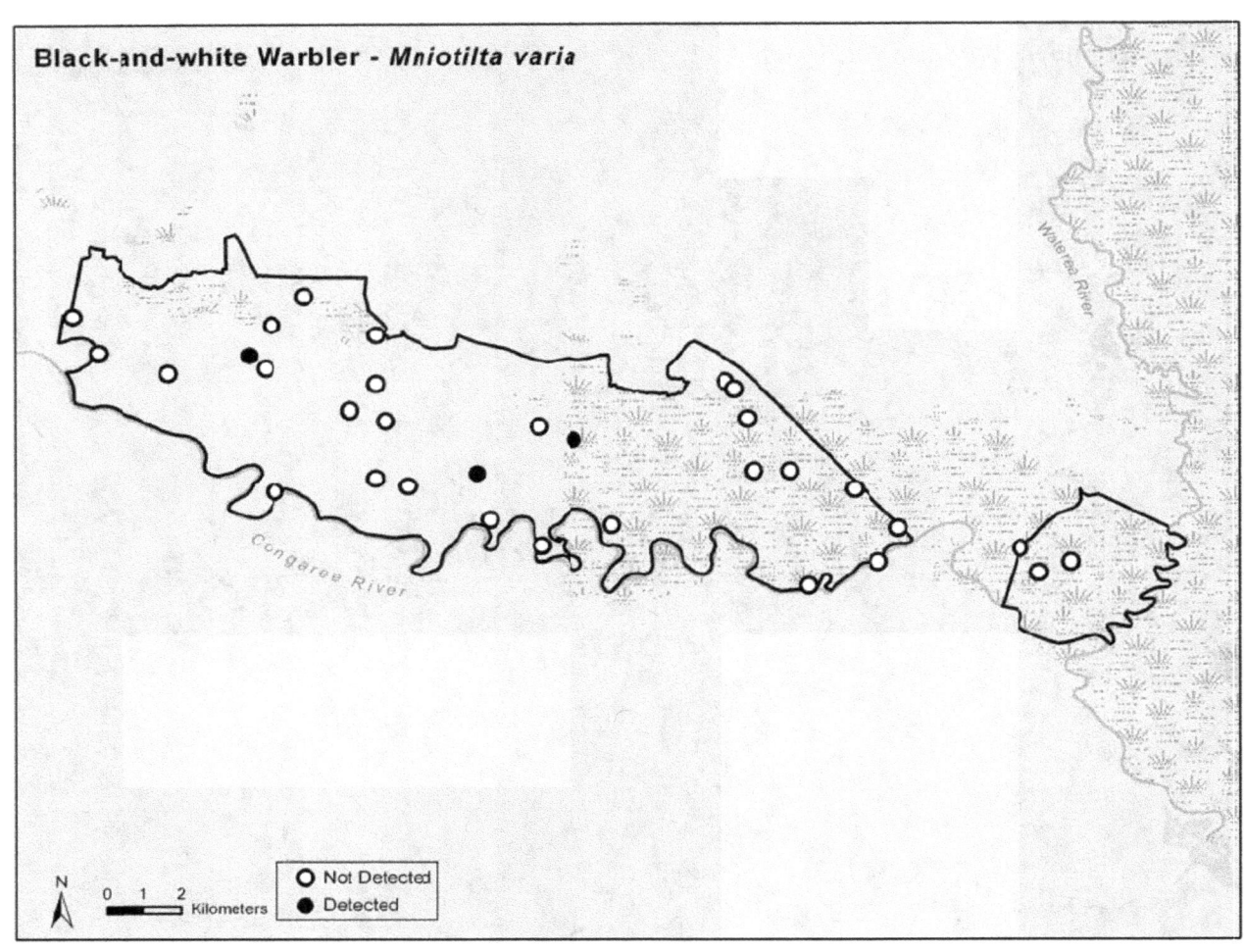

Figure D·9. Sampling locations where Black-and-white War ler (*Mniotilta varia*) was detected at CONG, 2009. ● = detected, ○ = not detected.

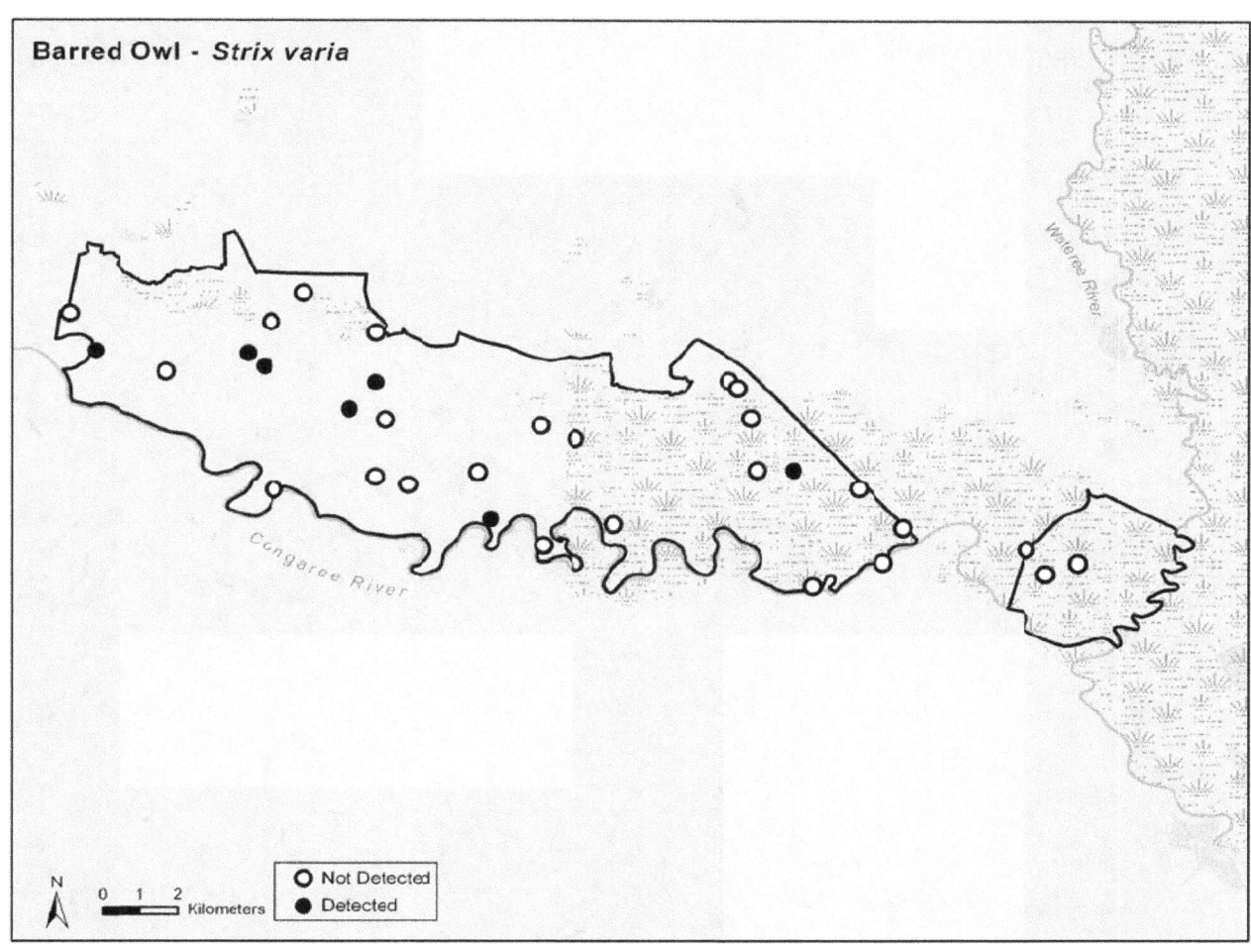

Figure D-10. Sampling locations where Barred Owl (*Strix varia*) was detected at CONG, 2009. ● = detected, ○ = not detected.

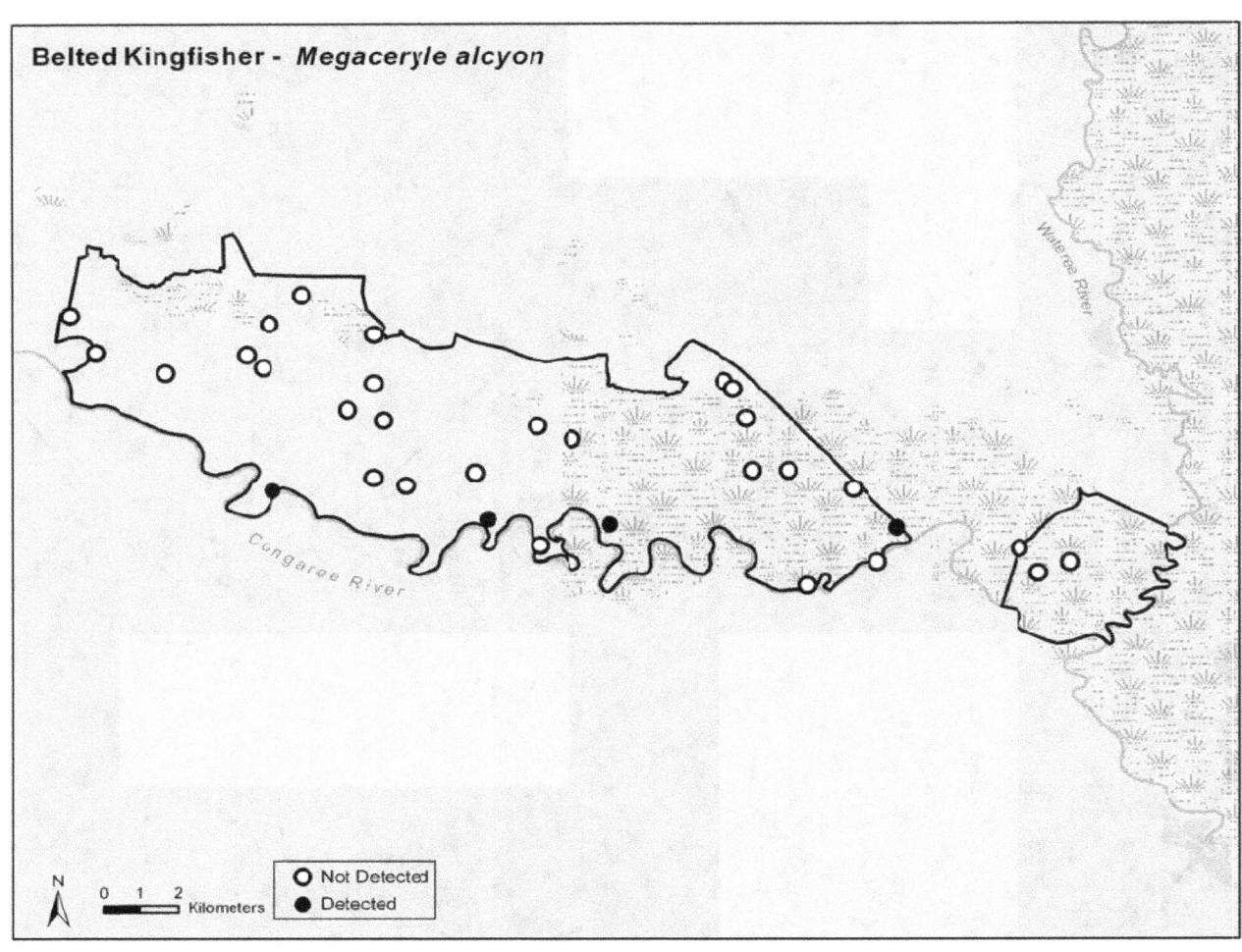

Figure D-11. Sampling locations where Belted Kingfisher (*Megaceryle al :yon*) was detected at CONG, 2009. ● = detected, ○ = not detected.

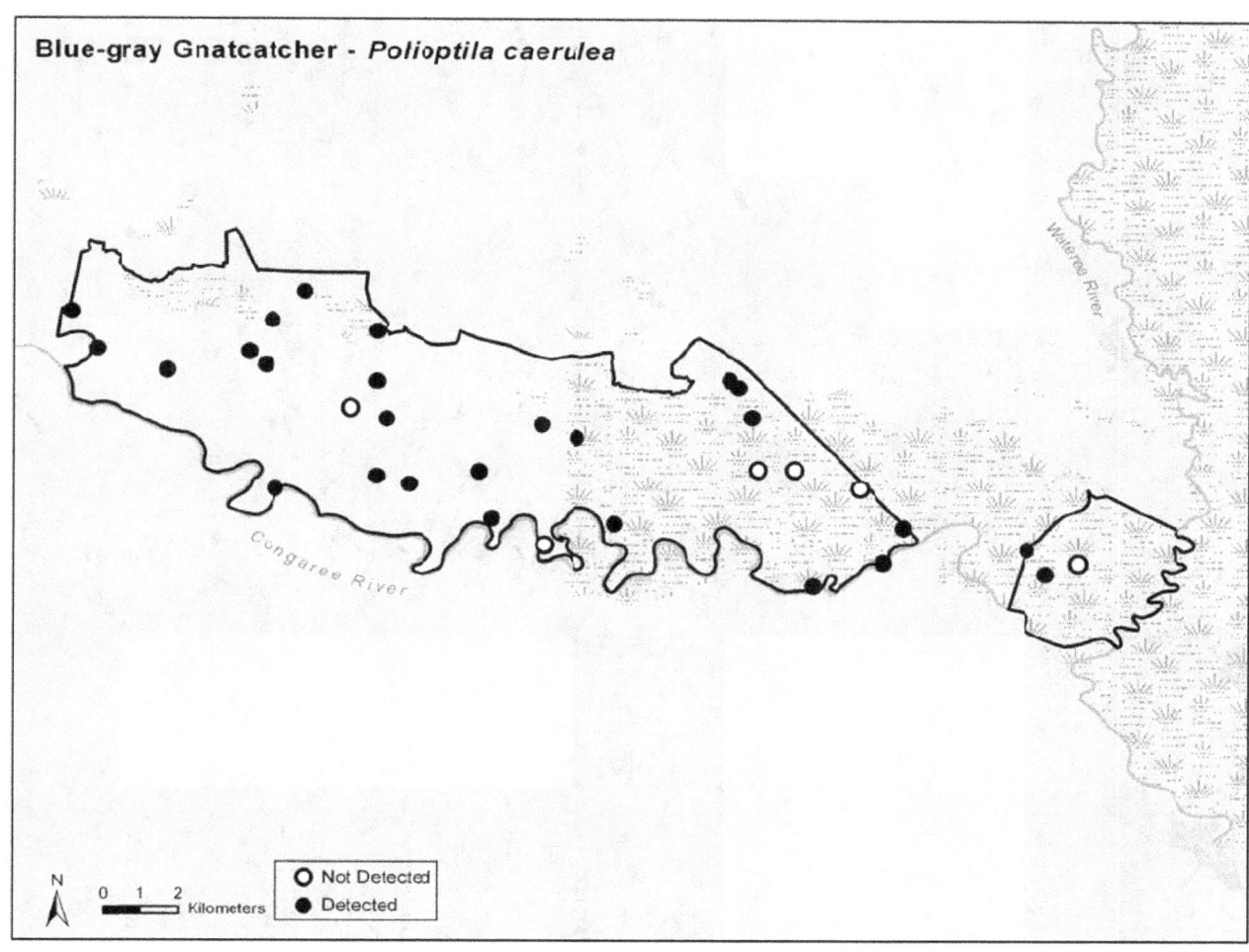

Figure D-12. Sampling locations where Blue-gray Gnatcatcher (*Polioptila caerulea*) was detected at CONG, 2009. ● = det cted, ○ = not detected.

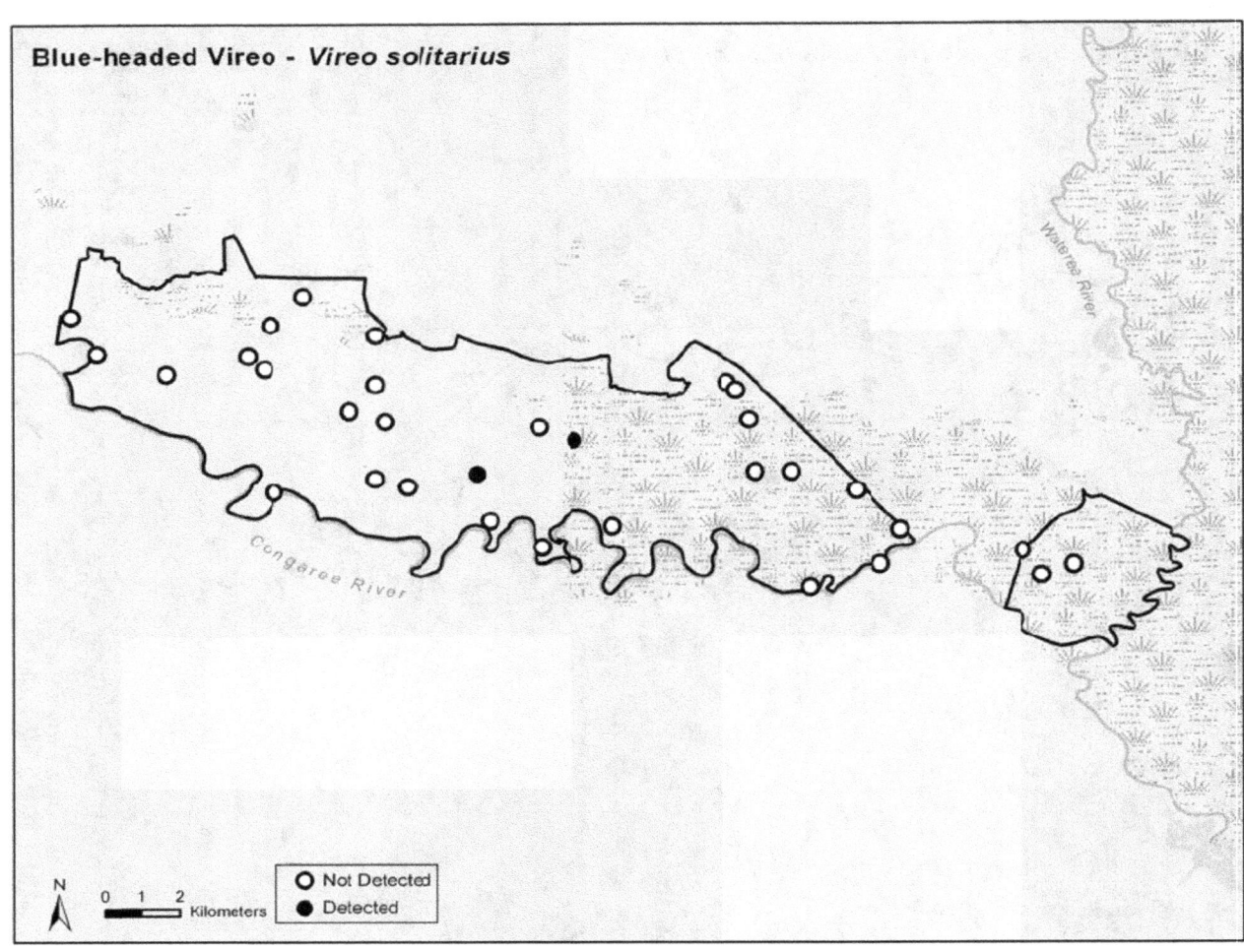

Figure D-13. Sampling locations where Blue-headed Vireo (*Vireo salitari is*) was detected at CONG, 2009. ● = detected, ○ = not detected.

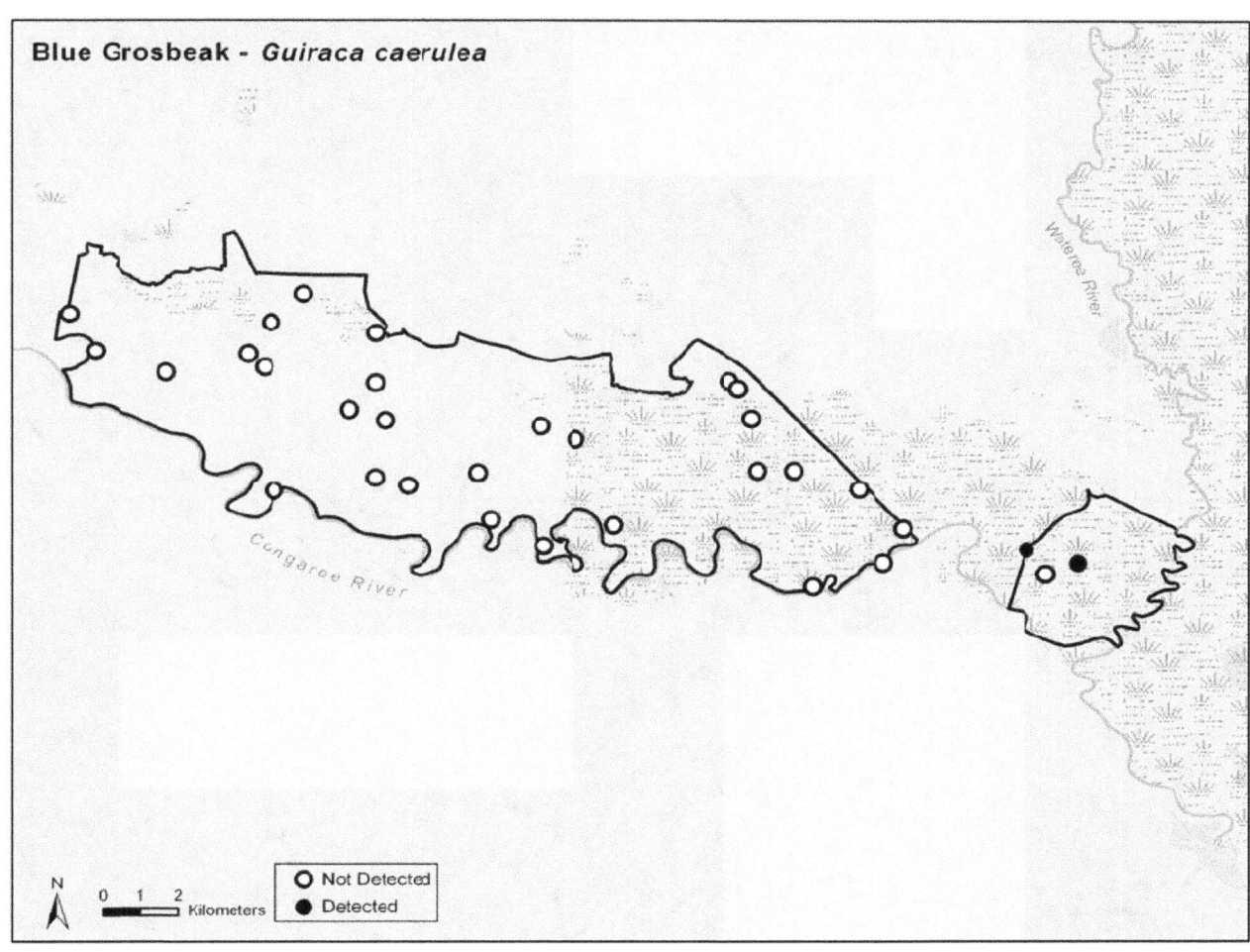

Figure D-14. Sampling locations where Blue Grosbeak (*Guiraca caerulea*) was detected at CONG, 2009. ● = detected, ○ = not detected.

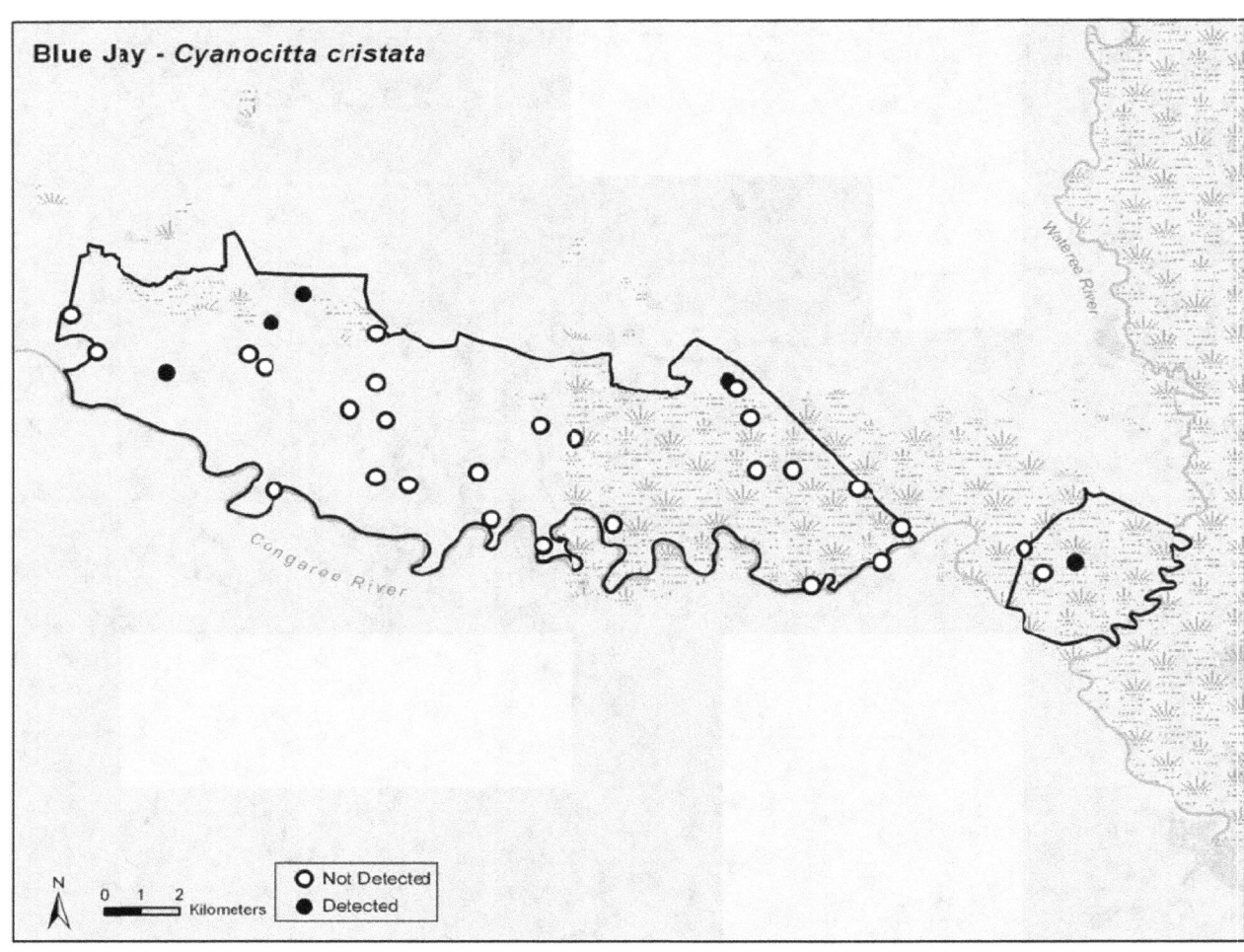

Figure D-15. Sampling locations where Blue Jay (*Cyanocitta cristata*) was detected at CONG, 2009. ● = detected, ○ = not detected.

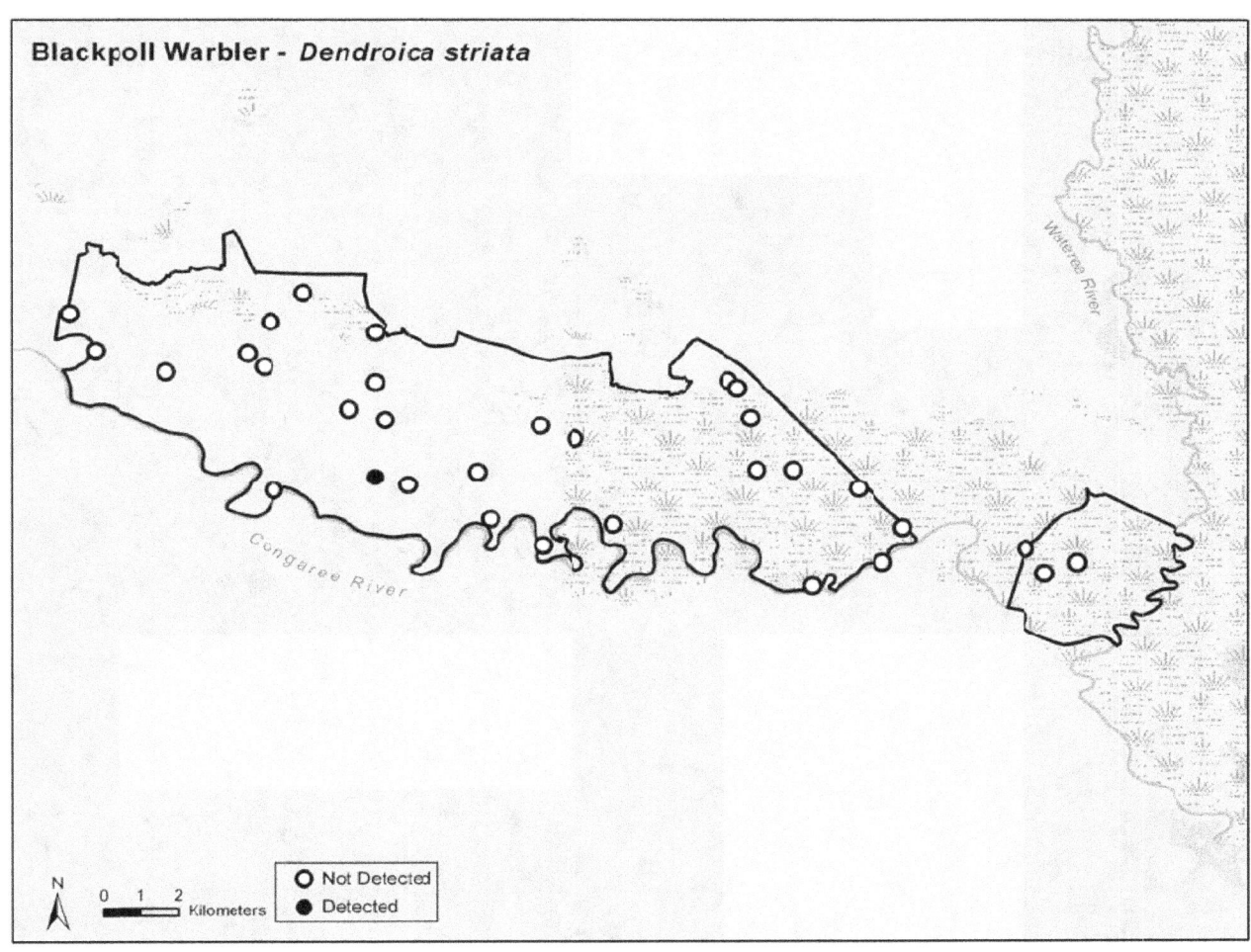

Figure D-16. Sampling locations where Blackpoll Warbler (*endroica striata*) was detected at CONG, 2009. • = detected, ○ = not detected.

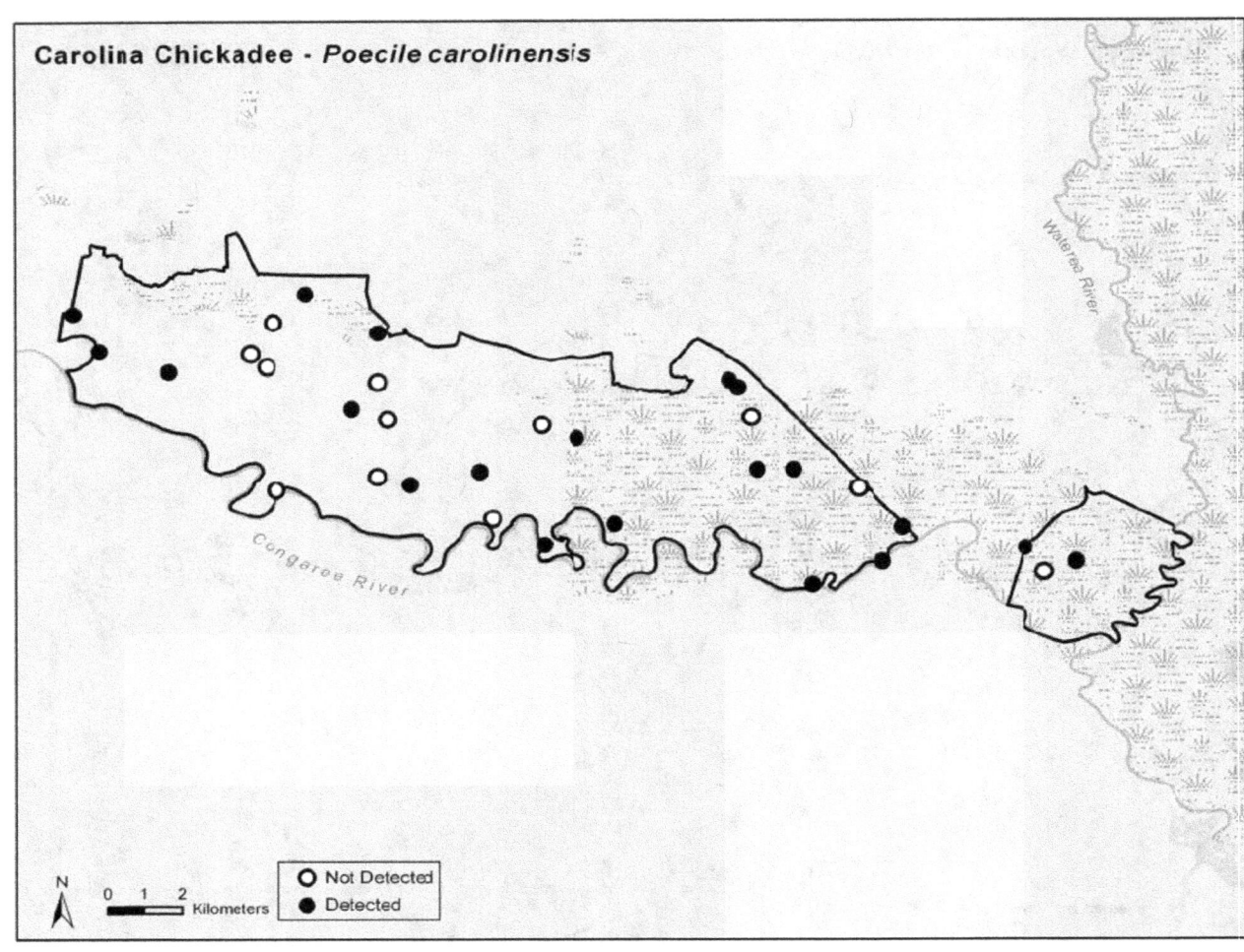

Figure D·17. Sampling locations where Carolina Chickadee (*Poecile car linensis*) was detected at CONG, 2009. • = det cted, ○ = not detected.

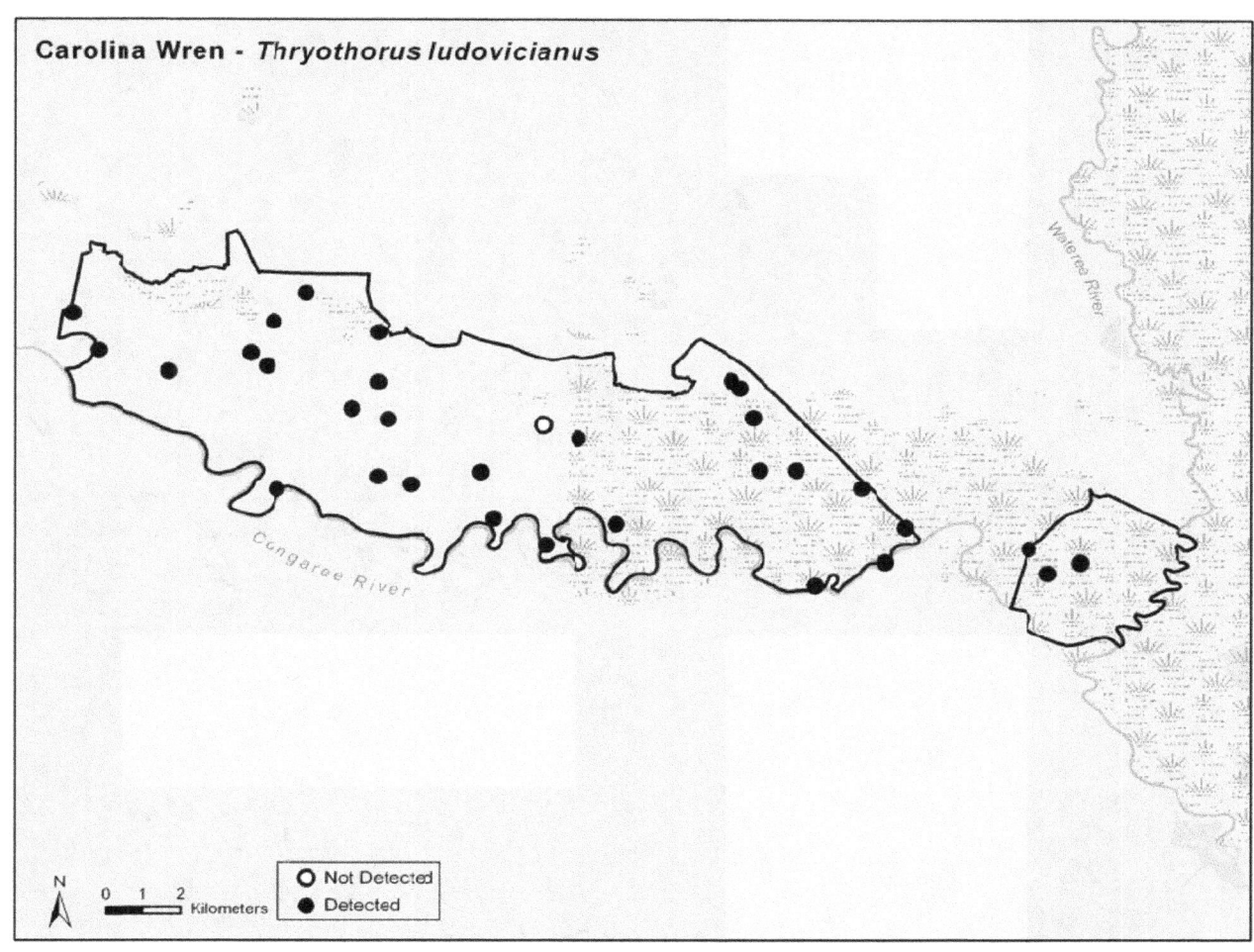

Figure D-18. Sampling locations where Carolina Wren (*Thryothorus ludo /icianus*) was detected at CONG, 2009. ● = det cted, ○ = not detected.

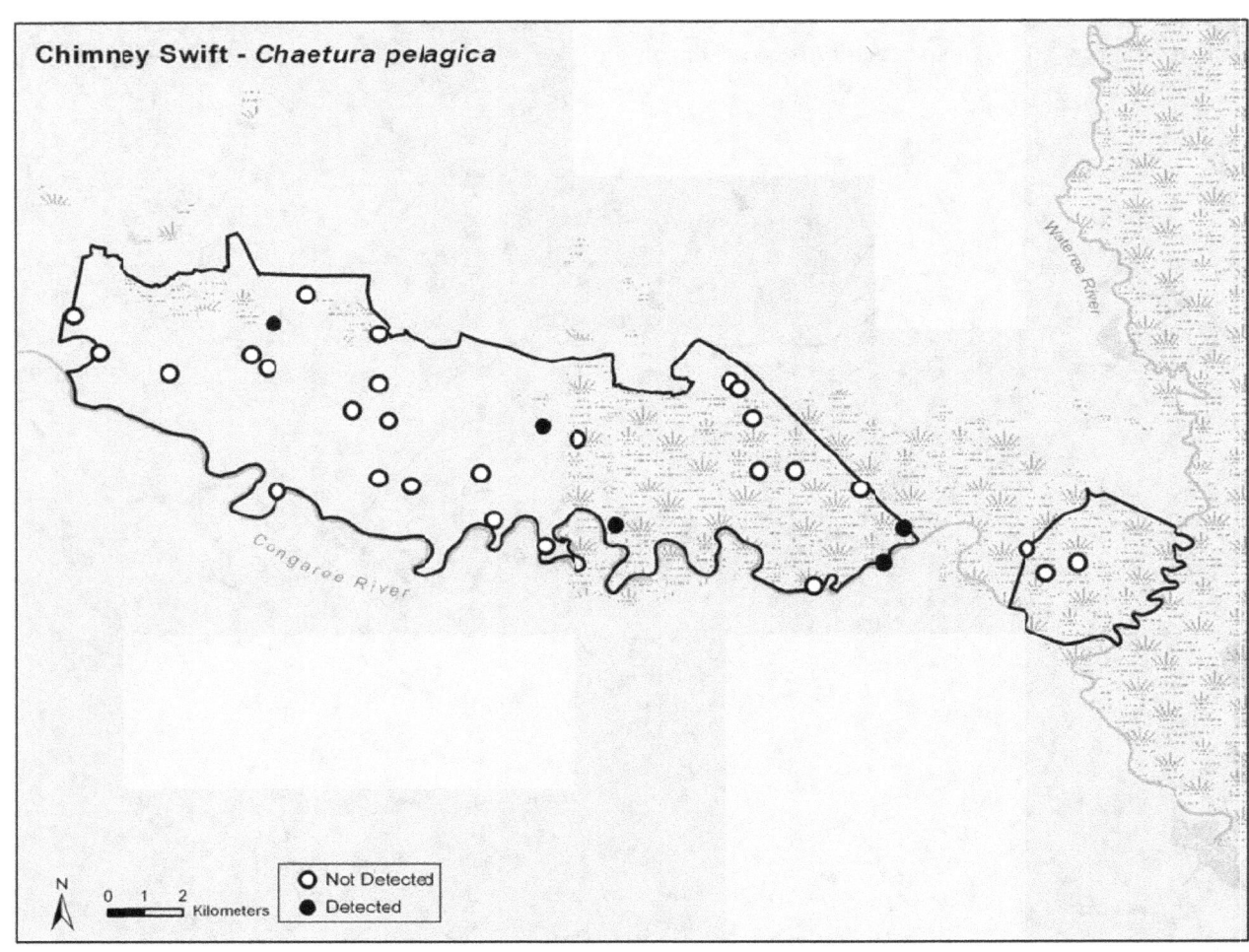

Figure D-19. Sampling locations where Chimney Swift (*Chaetura pelagica*) was detected at CONG, 2009. ● = detected, ○ = not detected.

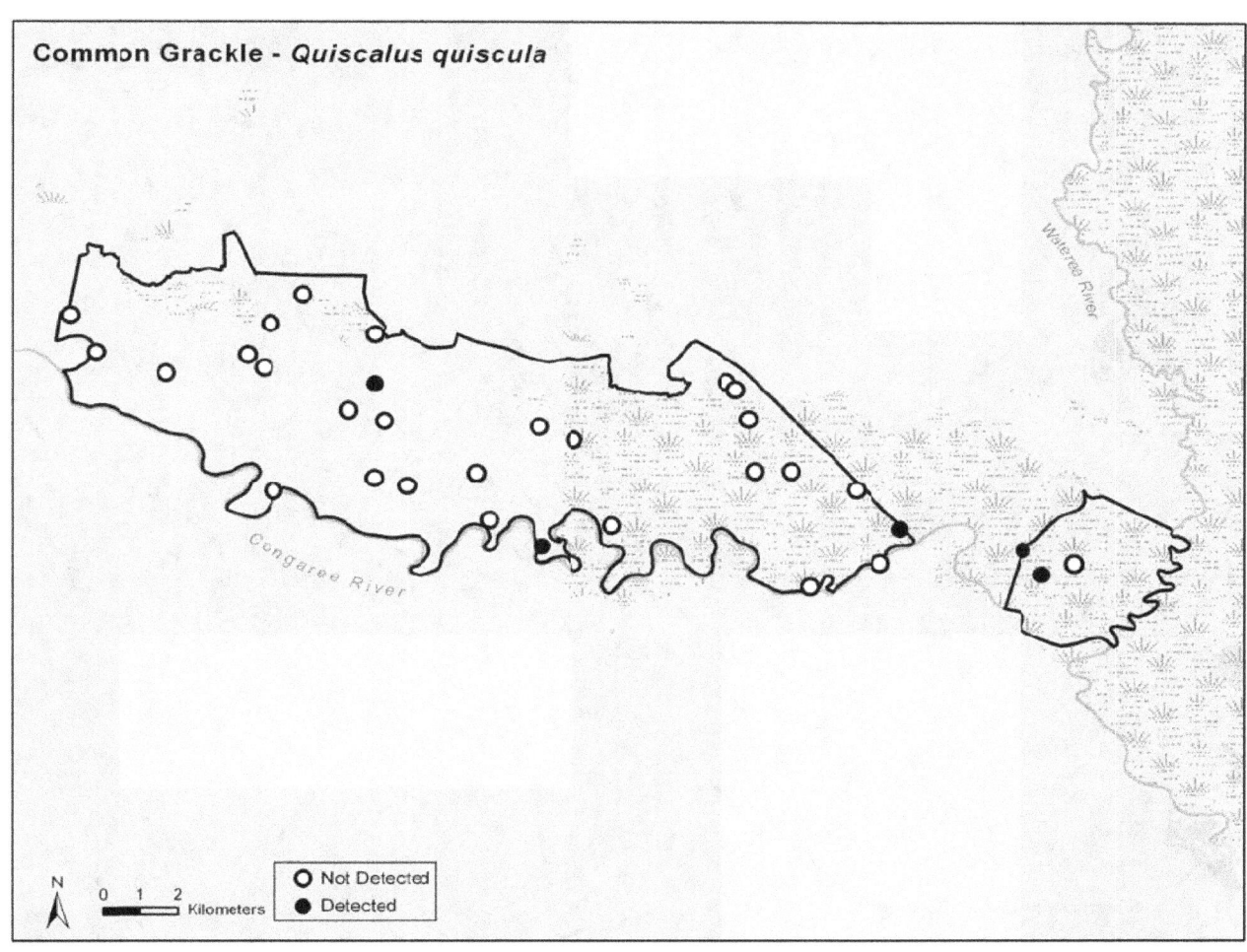

Figure D-20 Sampling locations where Common Grackle (*Quiscalus quiscula*) was detected at CONG, 2009. ● = detected, ○ = not detected.

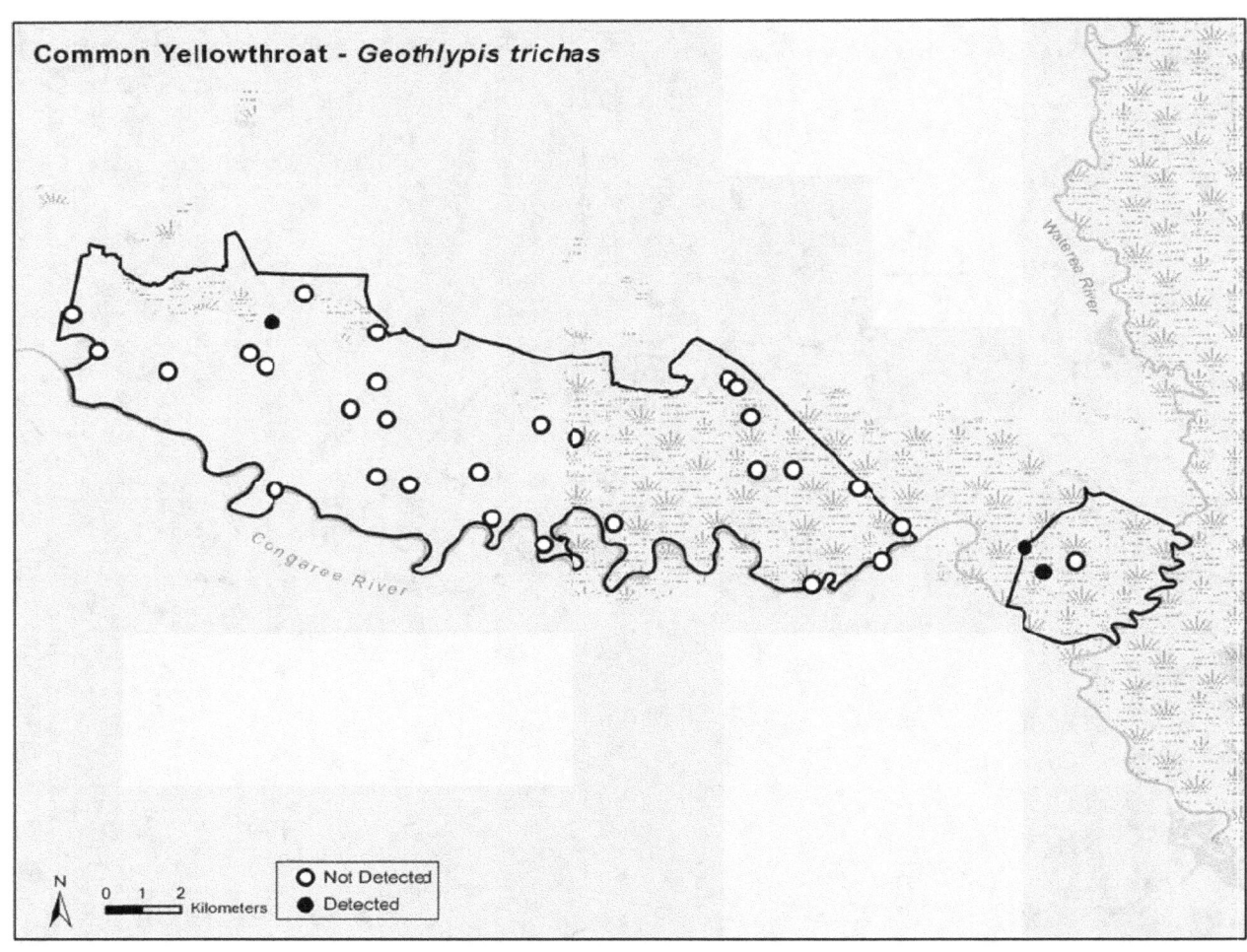

Figure D-21. Sampling locations where Common Yellowthroat (*Geothlypis trichas*) was detected at CONG, 2009. ● = det cted, ○ = not detected.

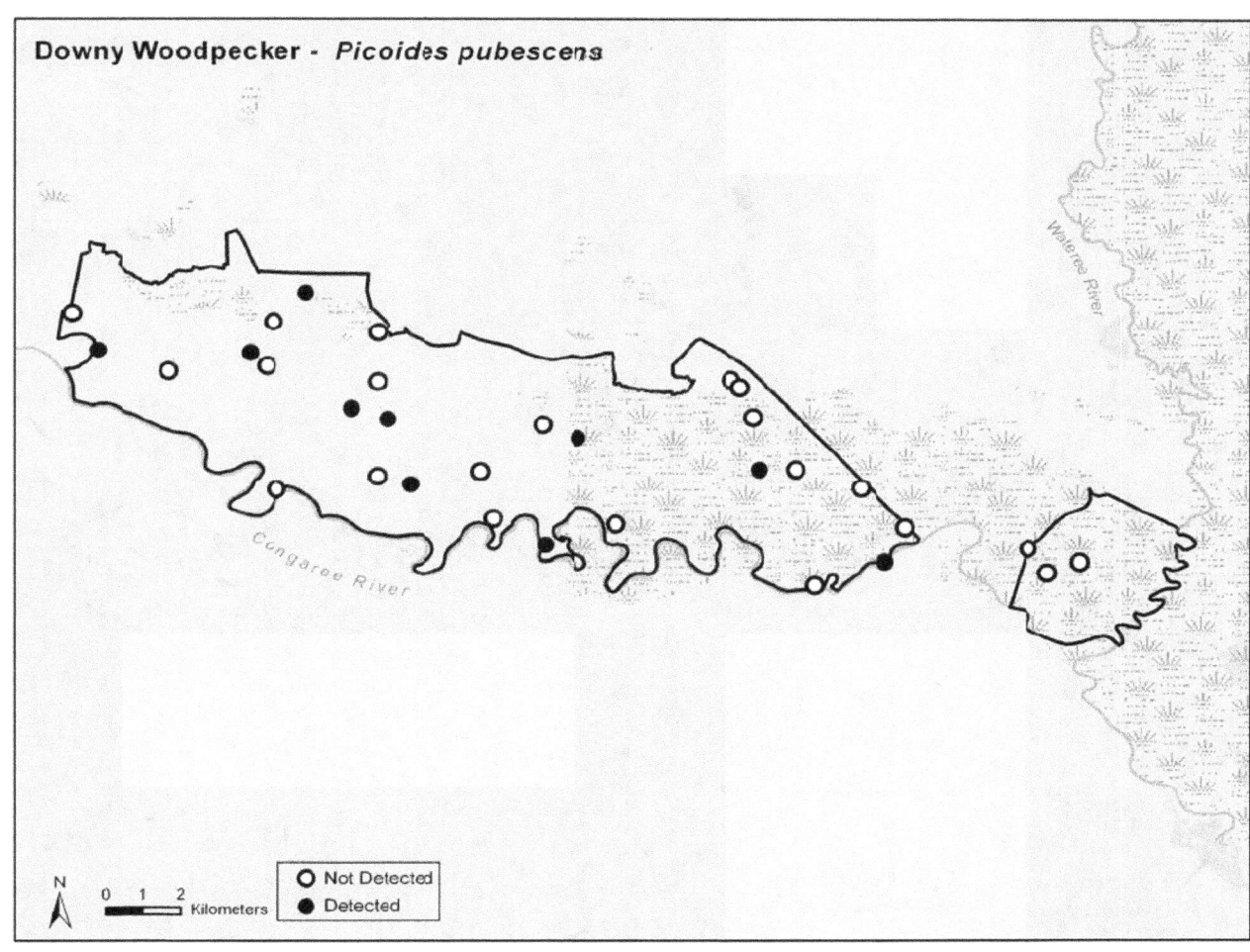

Figure D-22. Sampling locations where Downy Woodpecker (*Picoides pubescens*) was detected at CONG, 2009. ● = det cted, ○ = not detected.

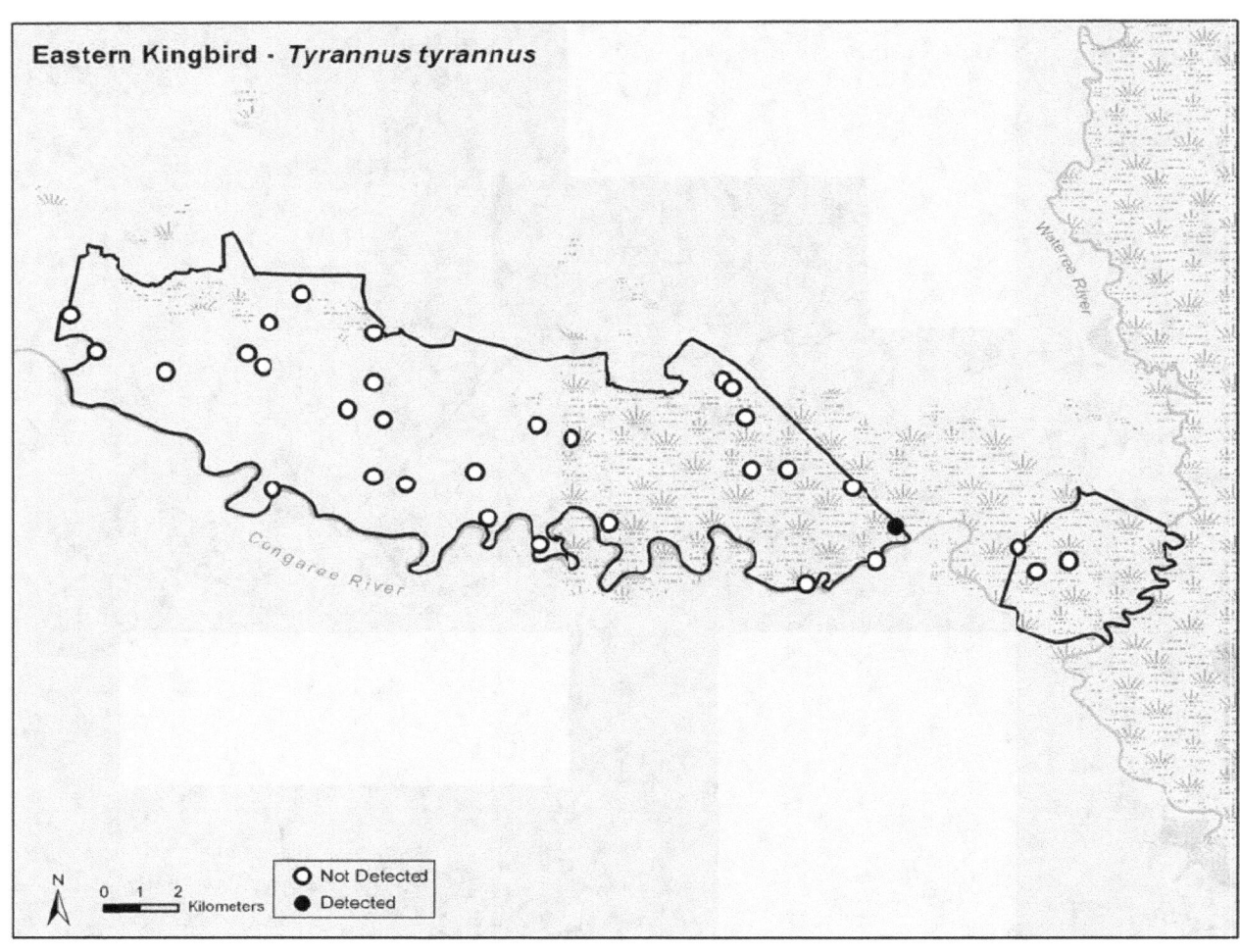

Figure D-23. Sampling locations where Eastern Kingbird (*T rannus tyrannus*) was detected at CONG, 2009. ● = detected, ○ = not detected.

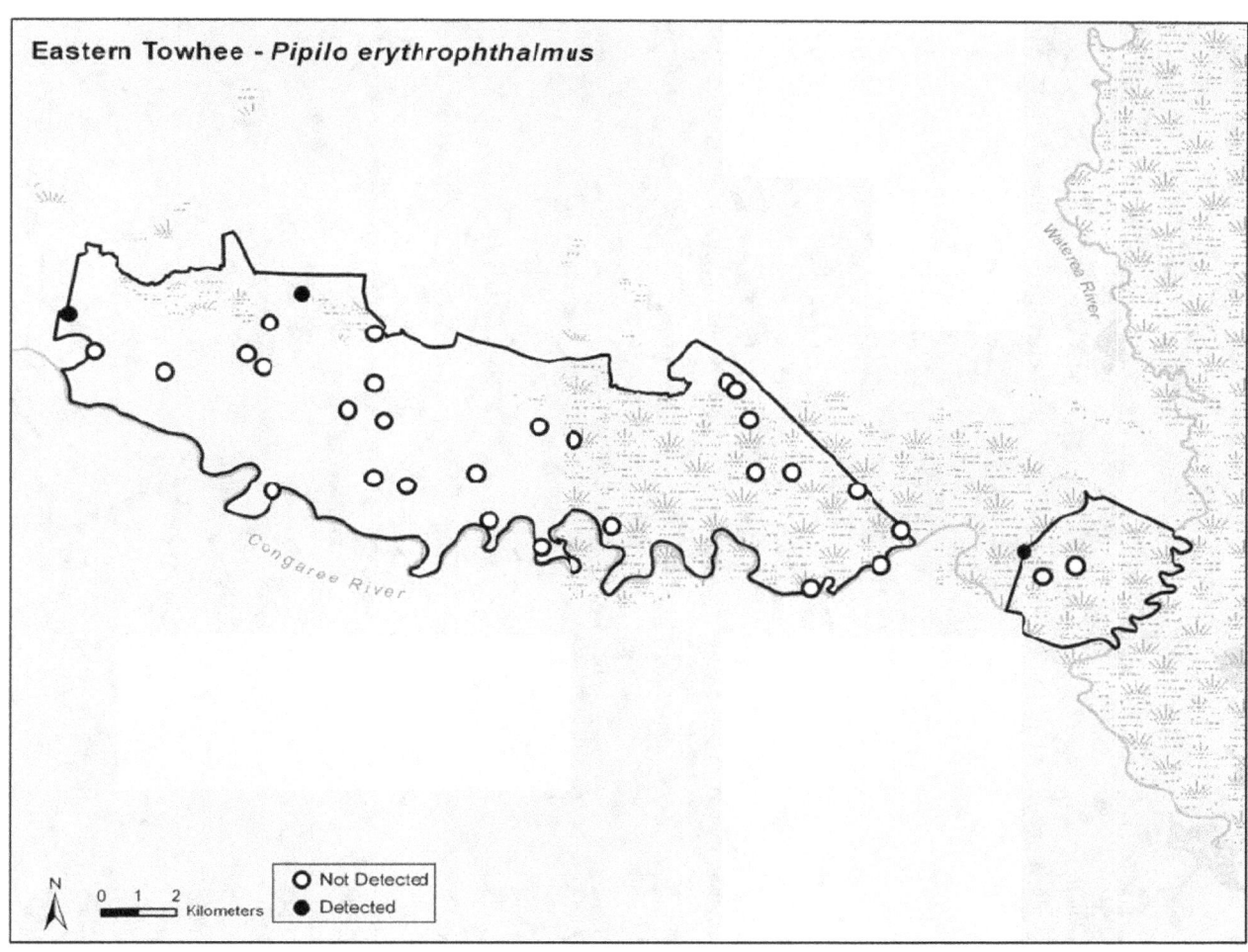

Figure D-24. Sampling locations where Eastern Towhee (*Pipilo erythrop thalmus*) was detected at CONG, 2009. ● = det cted, ○ = not detected.

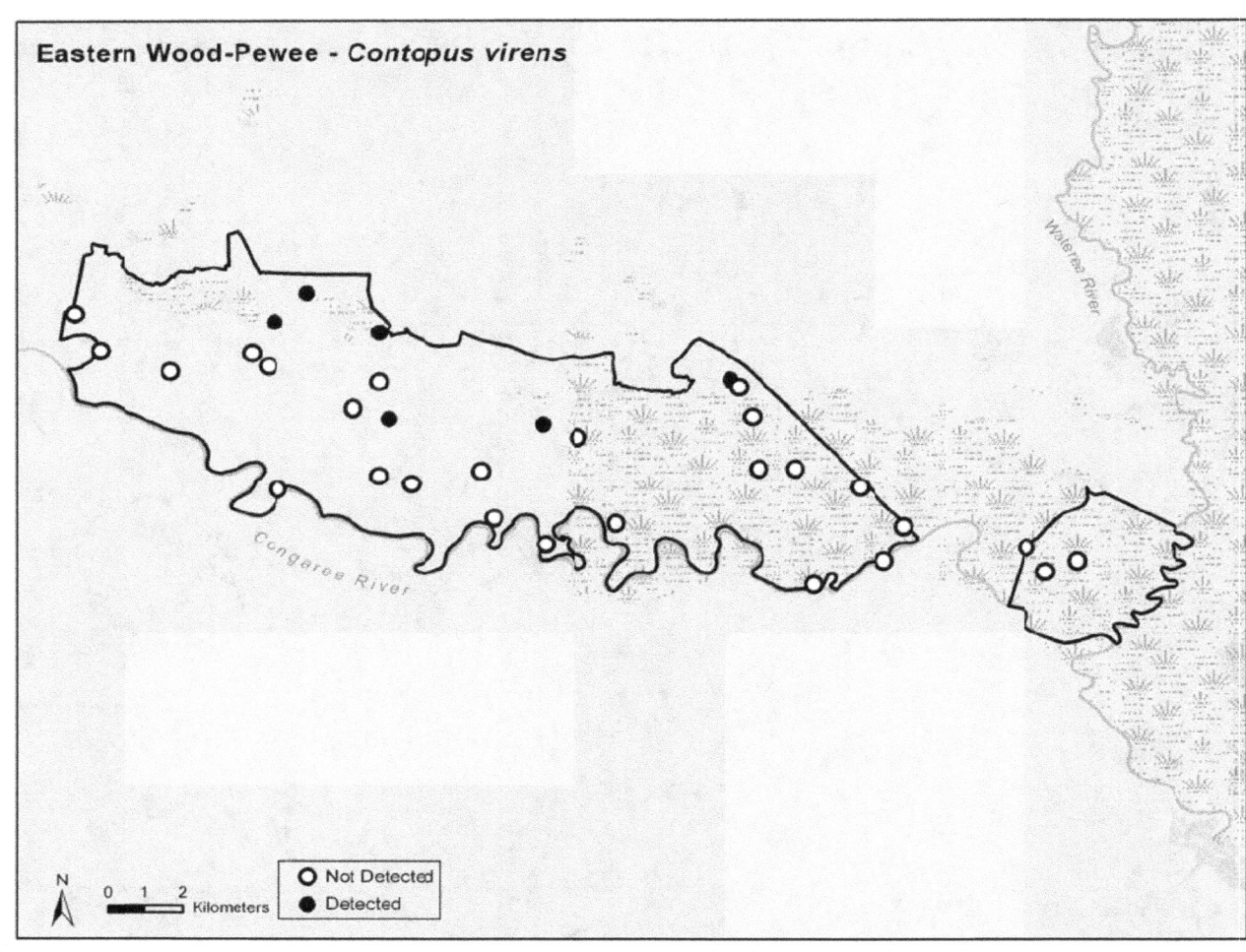

Figure D-25. Sampling locations where Eastern Wood-Pew e (*Contopus virens*) was detected at CONG, 2009. ● = detected, ○ = not detected.

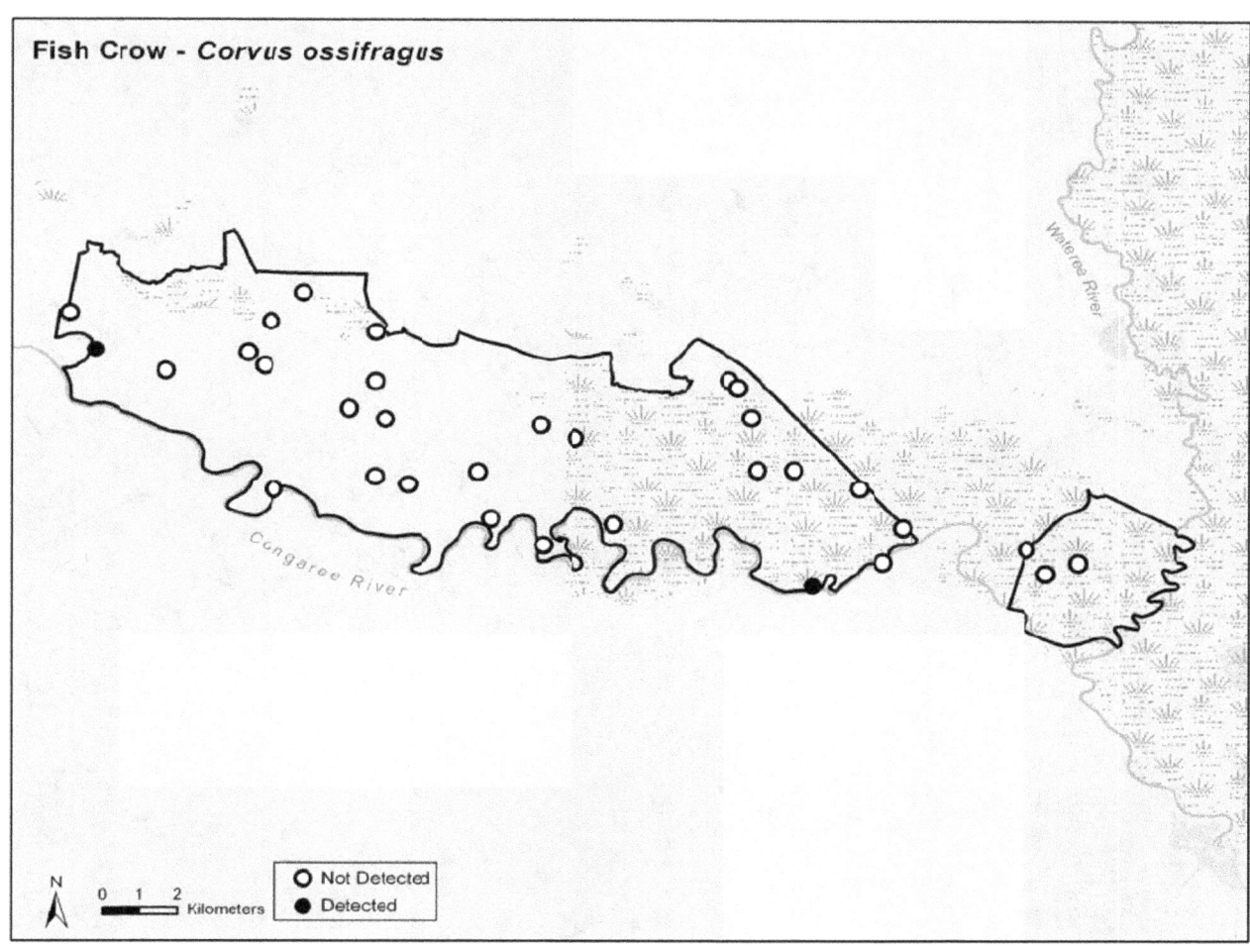

Figure D-26. Sampling locations where Fish Crow (*Corvus ossifragus*) was detected at CONG, 2009. ● = detected, ○ = not detected.

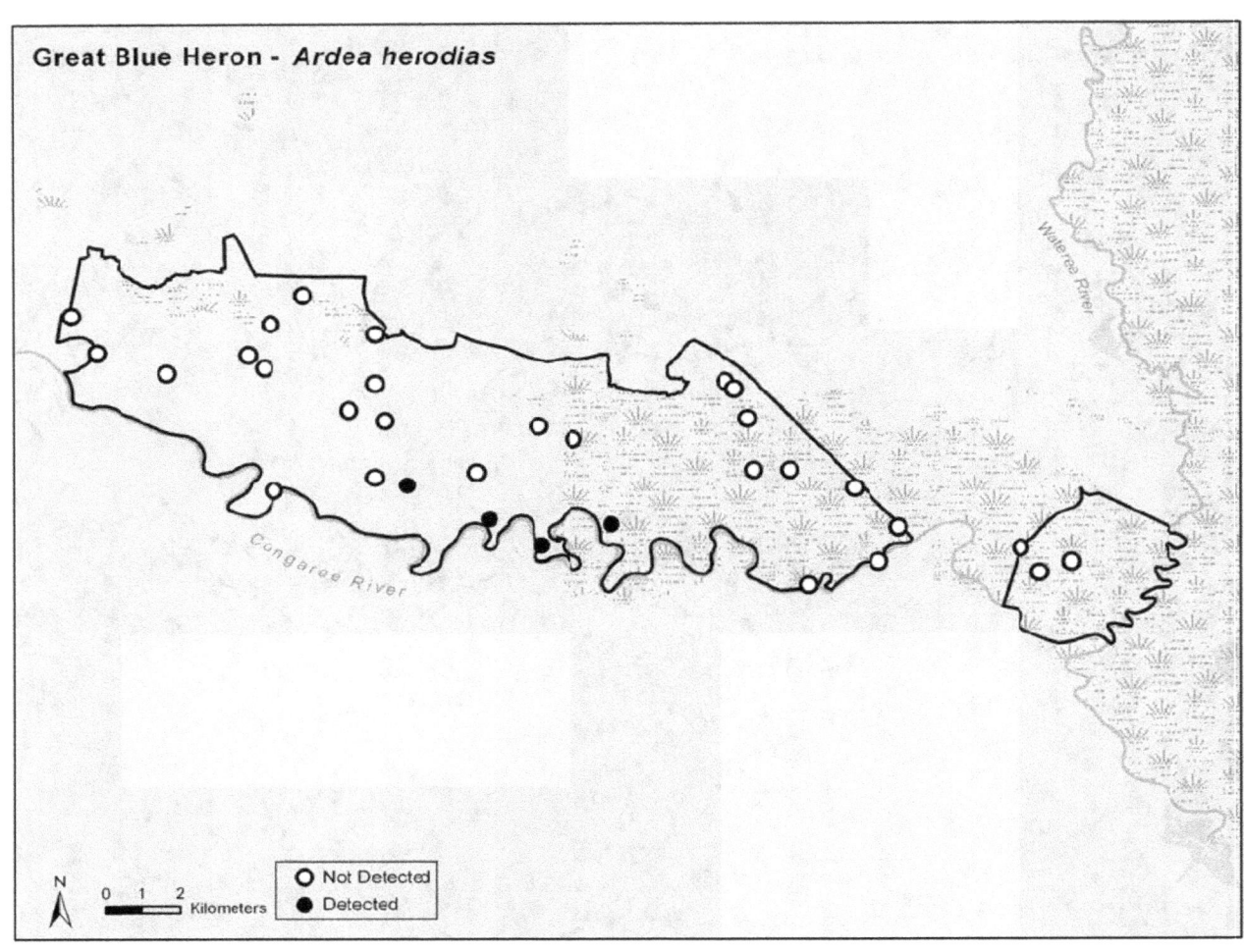

Figure D-27. Sampling locations where Great Blue Heron (*Ardea herodias*) was detected at CONG, 2009. ● = detected, ○ = not detected.

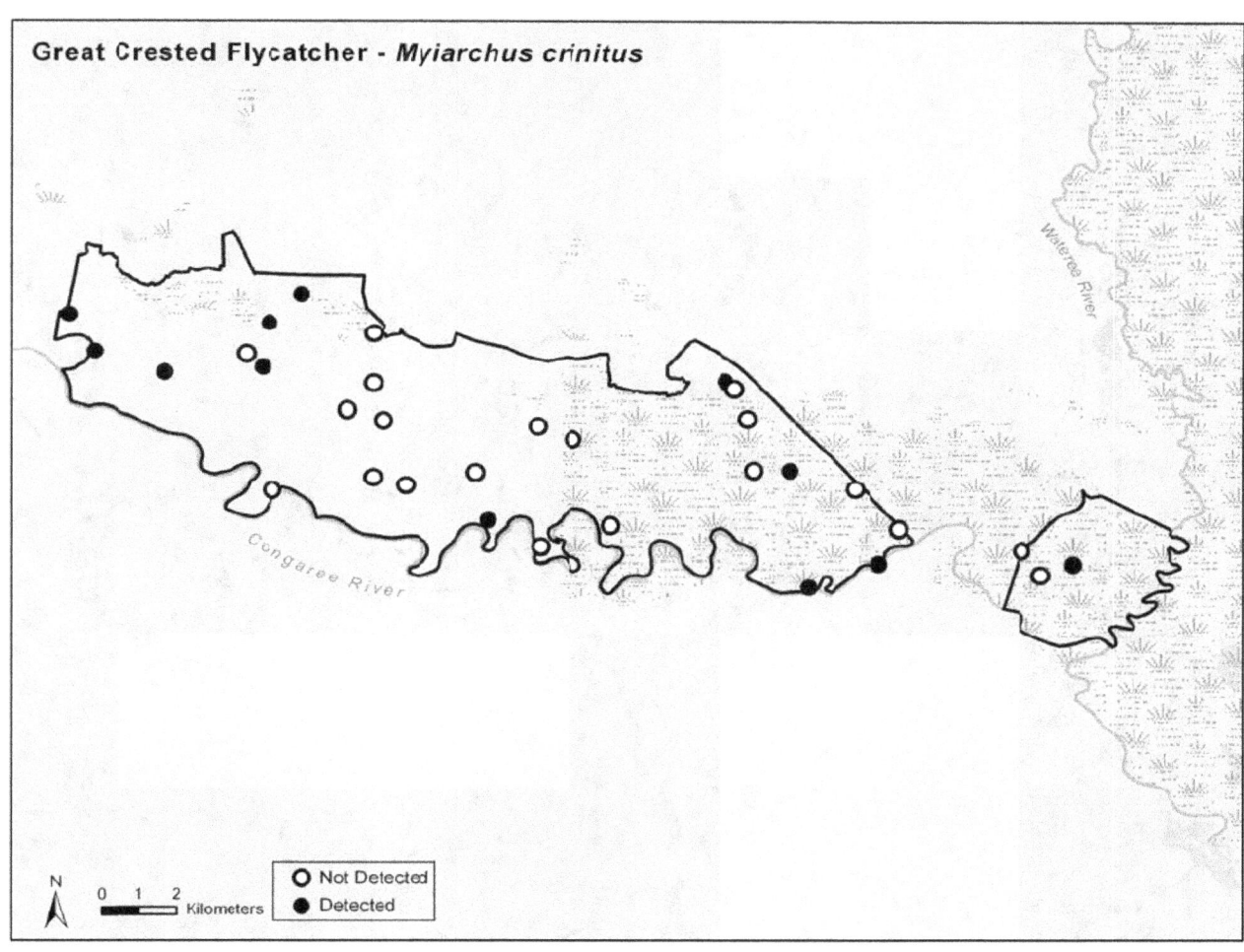

Figure D-28. Sampling locations where Great Crested Flycatcher (*Myiarchus crinitus*) was detected at CONG, 2009. ● = det cted, ○ = not detected.

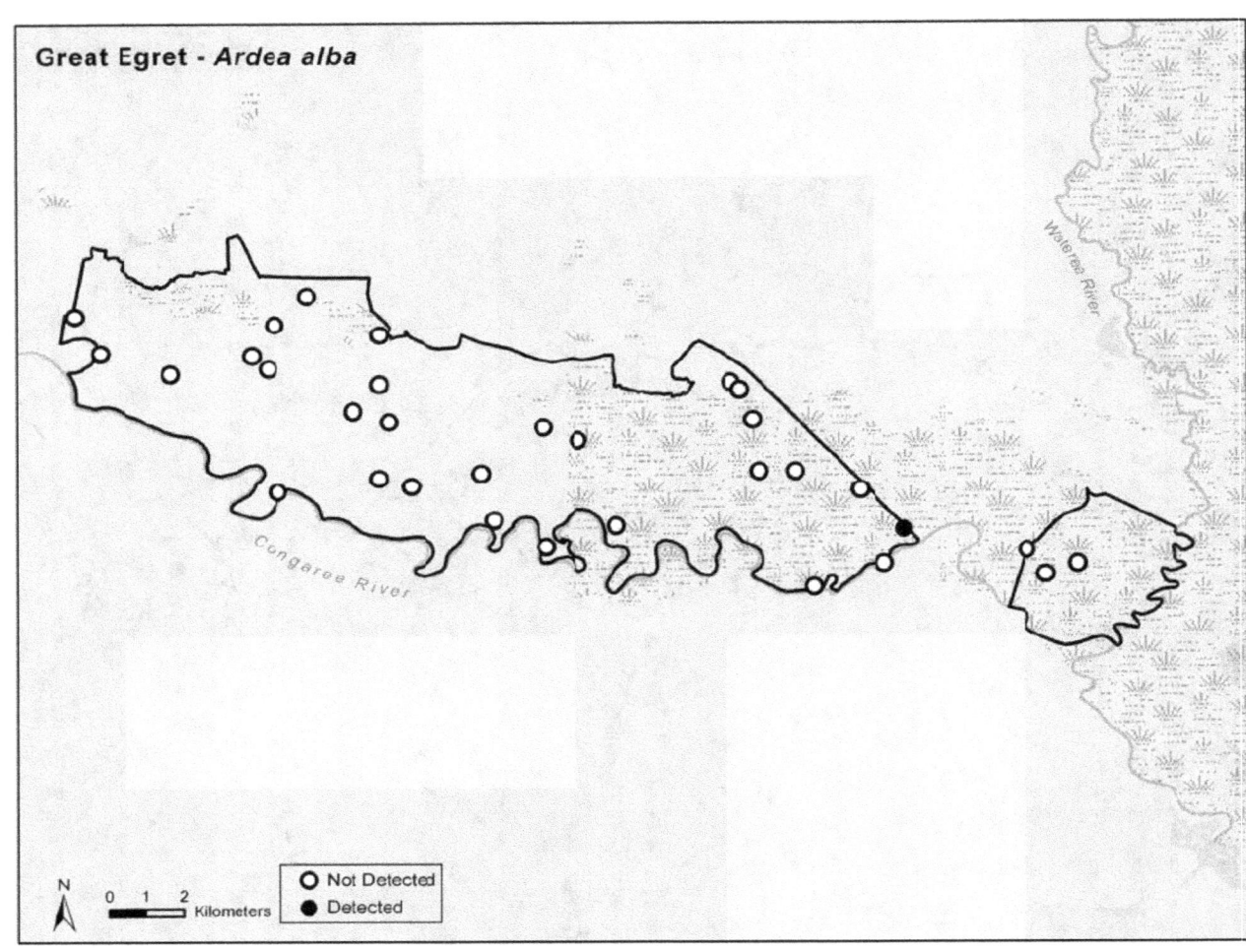

Figure D-29. Sampling locations where Great Egret (*Ardea alba*) was detected at CONG, 2009. ● = detected, ○ = not detected.

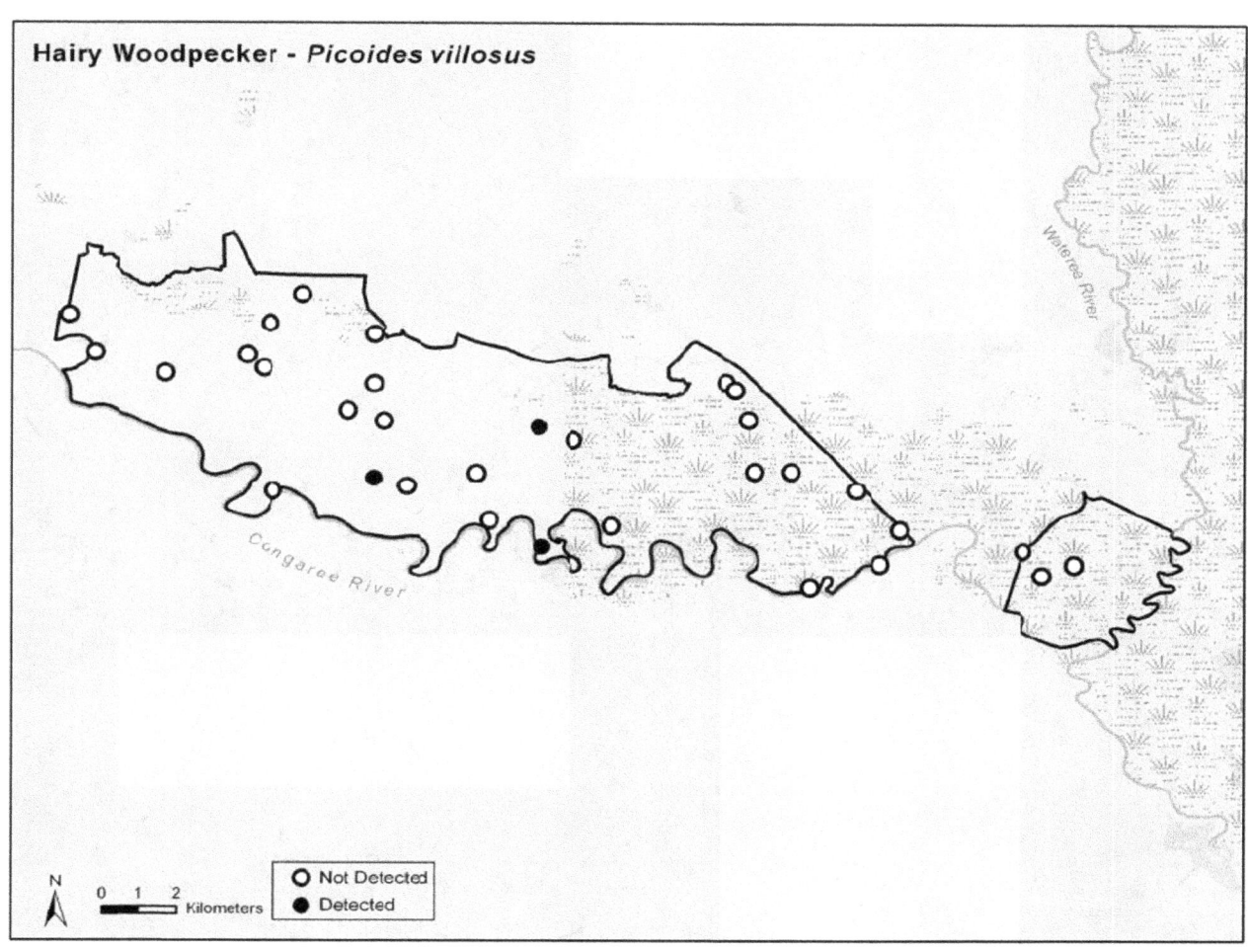

Figure D-30. Sampling locations where Hairy Woodpecker (*Picoides villosus*) was detected at CONG, 2009. ● = detected, ○ = not detected.

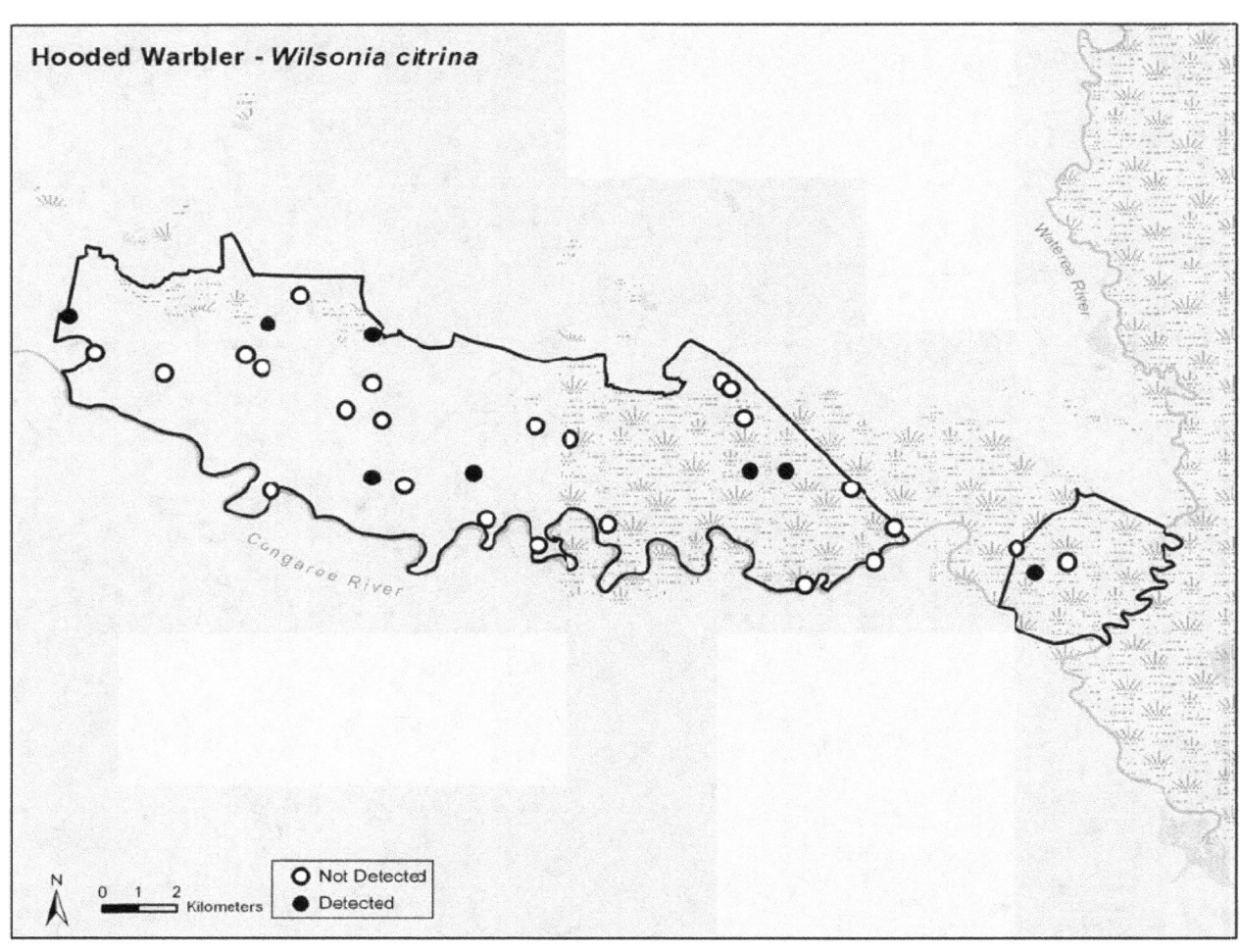

Figure D-31. Sampling locations where Hooded Warbler (*Wilsonia citrina*) was detected at CONG, 2009. ● = detected, ○ = not detected.

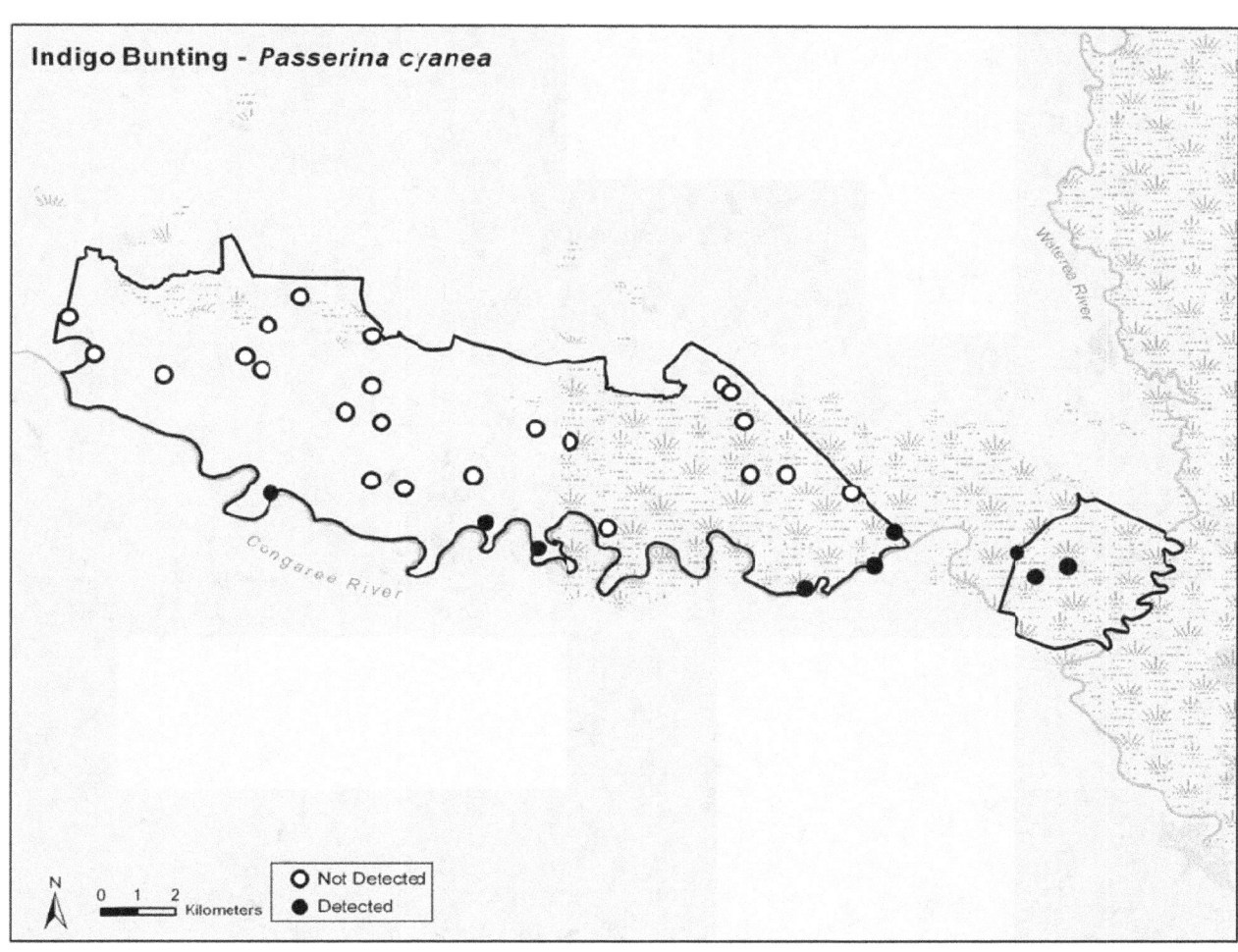

Figure D-32. Sampling locations where Indigo Bunting (*Passerina cyanea*) was detected at CONG, 2009. ● = detected, ○ = not detected.

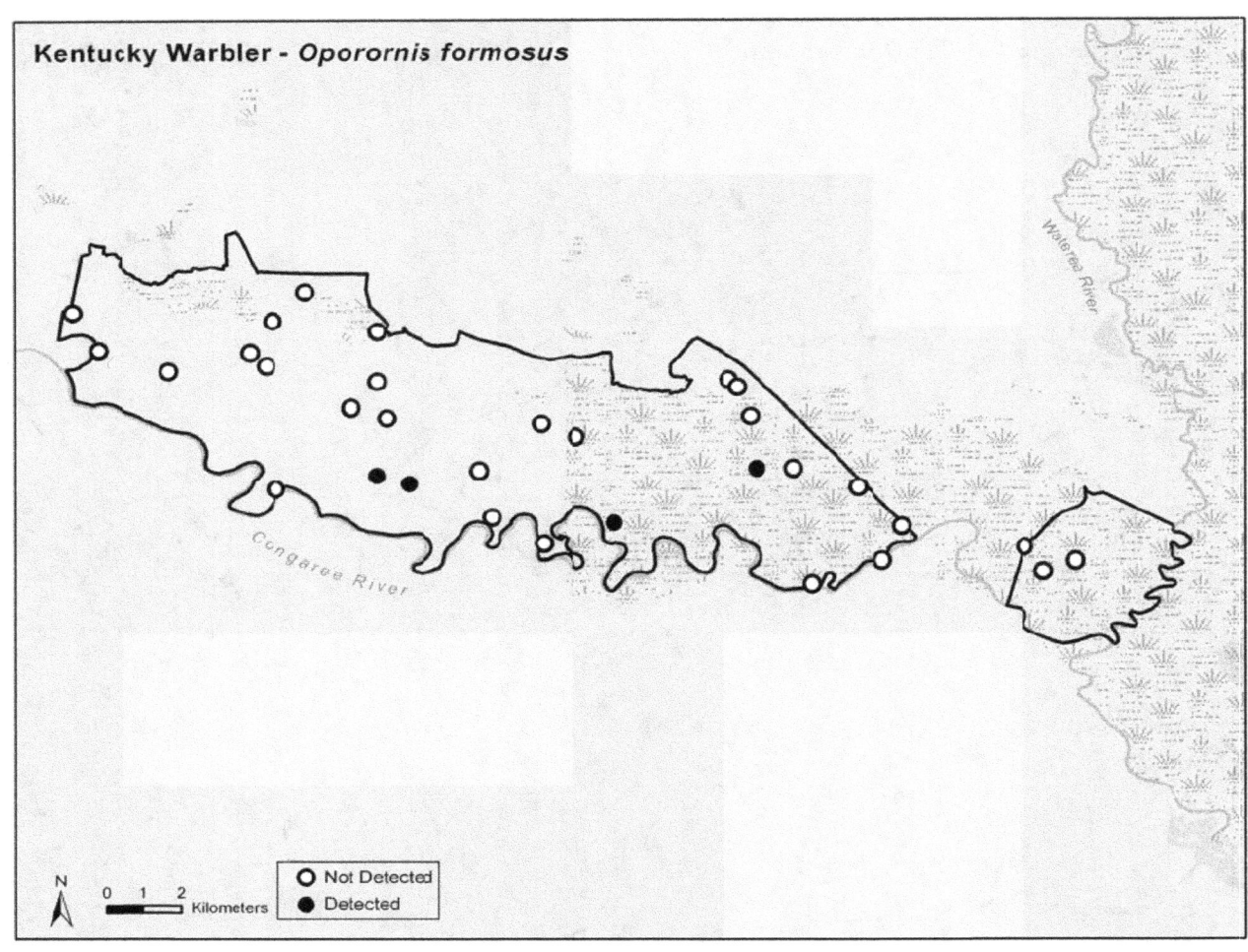

Figure D-33. Sampling locations where Kentucky Warbler (*Oporornis for nosus*) was detected at CONG, 2009. ● = detected, ○ = not detected.

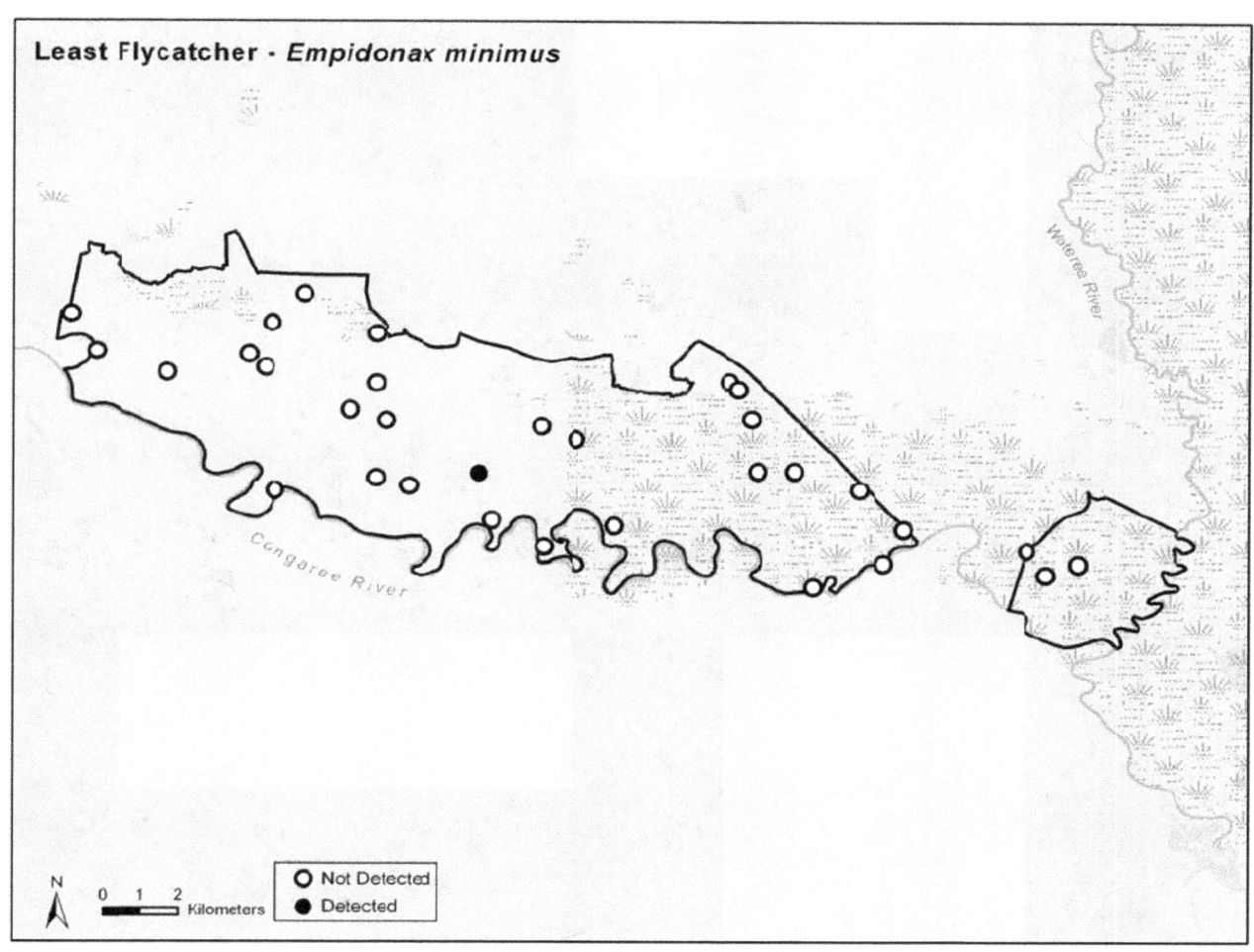

Figure D·34. Sampling locations where Least Flycatcher (E ìpidonax minimus) was detected at CONG, 2009. ● = detected, ○ = not detected.

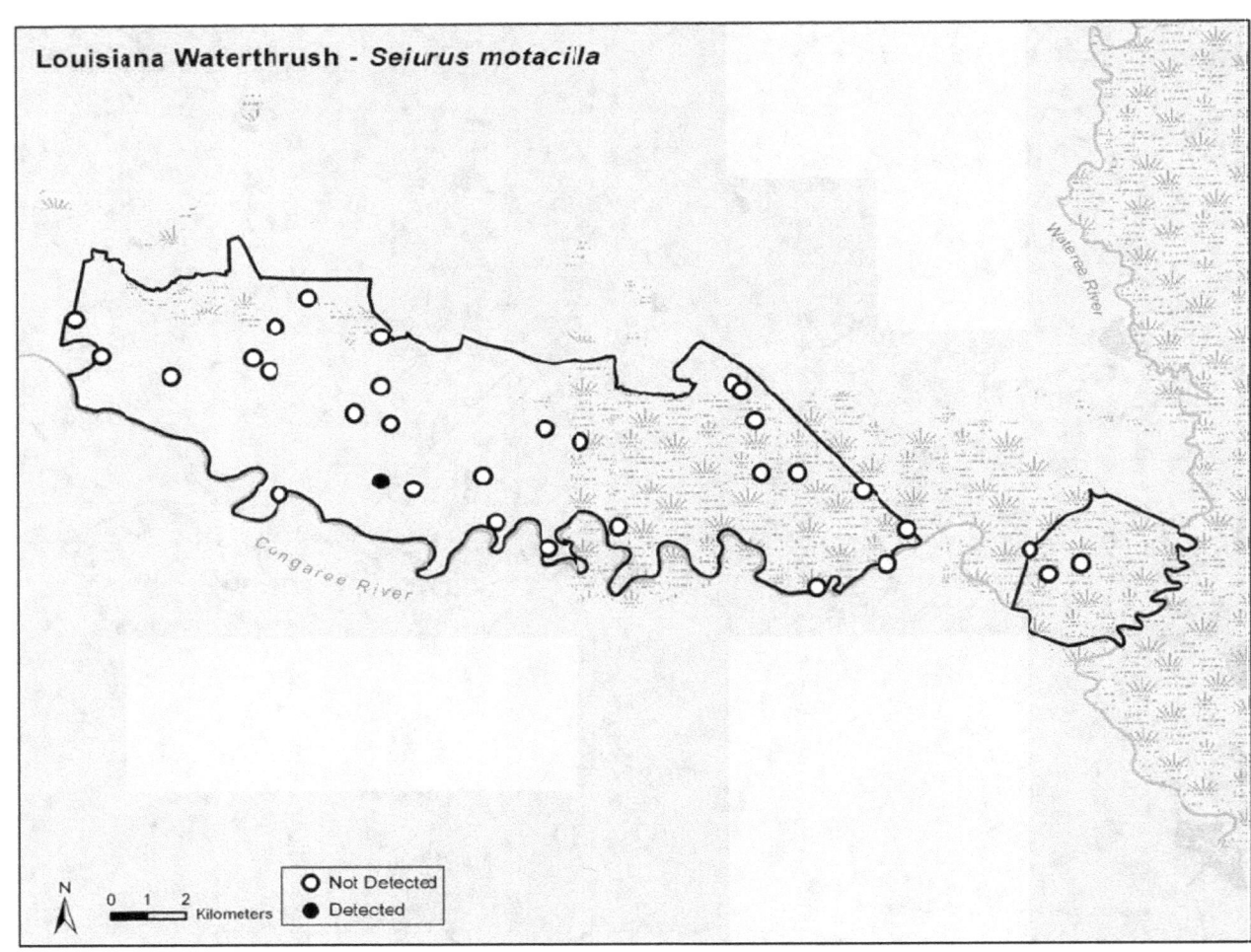

Figure D-35. Sampling locations where Louisiana Waterthrush (*Seiurus motacilla*) was detected at CONG, 2009. ● = det·cted, ○ = not detected.

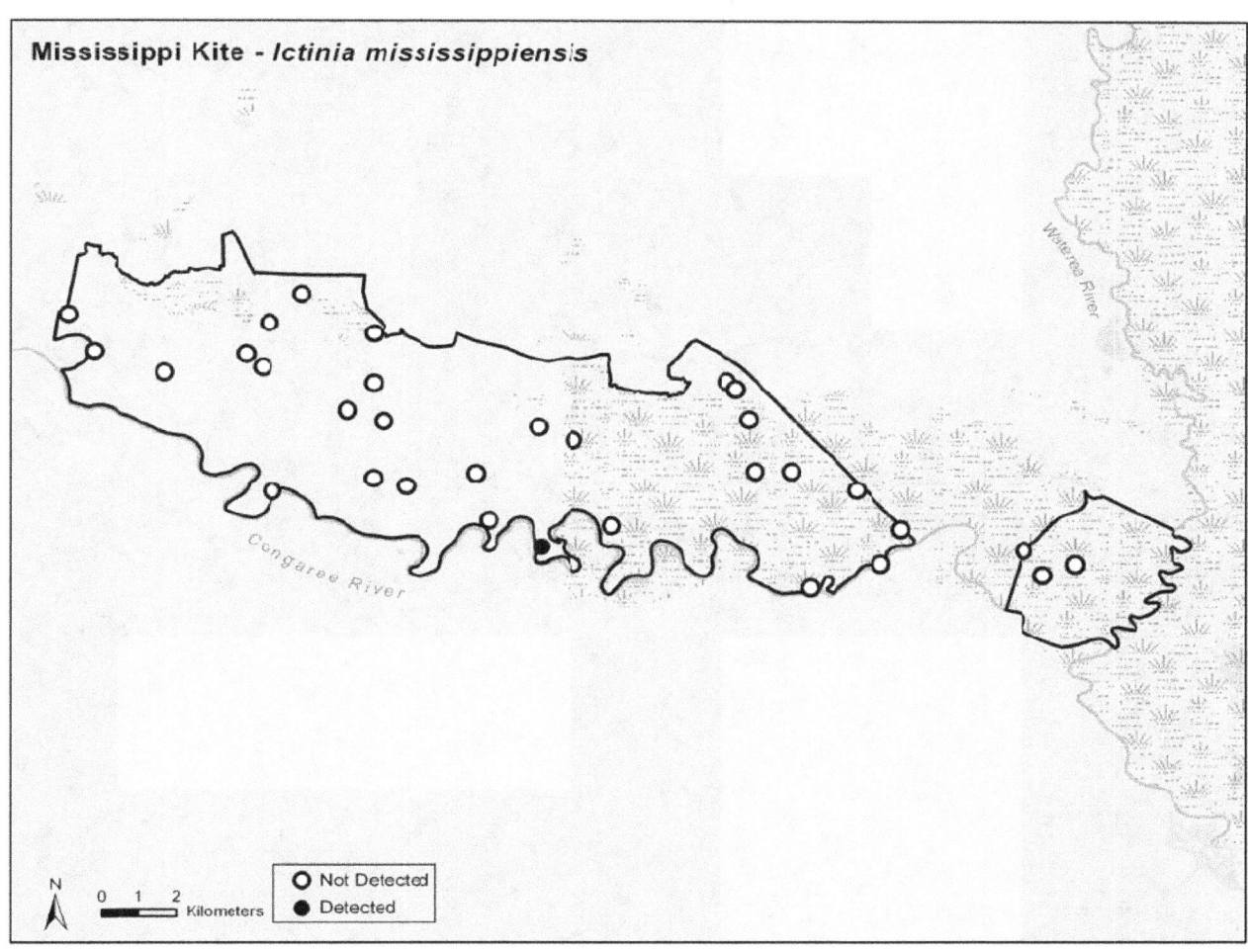

Figure D-36. Sampling locations where Mississippi Kite (*Icti ia mississip iensis*) was detected at CONG, 2009. • = detected, ○ = not detected.

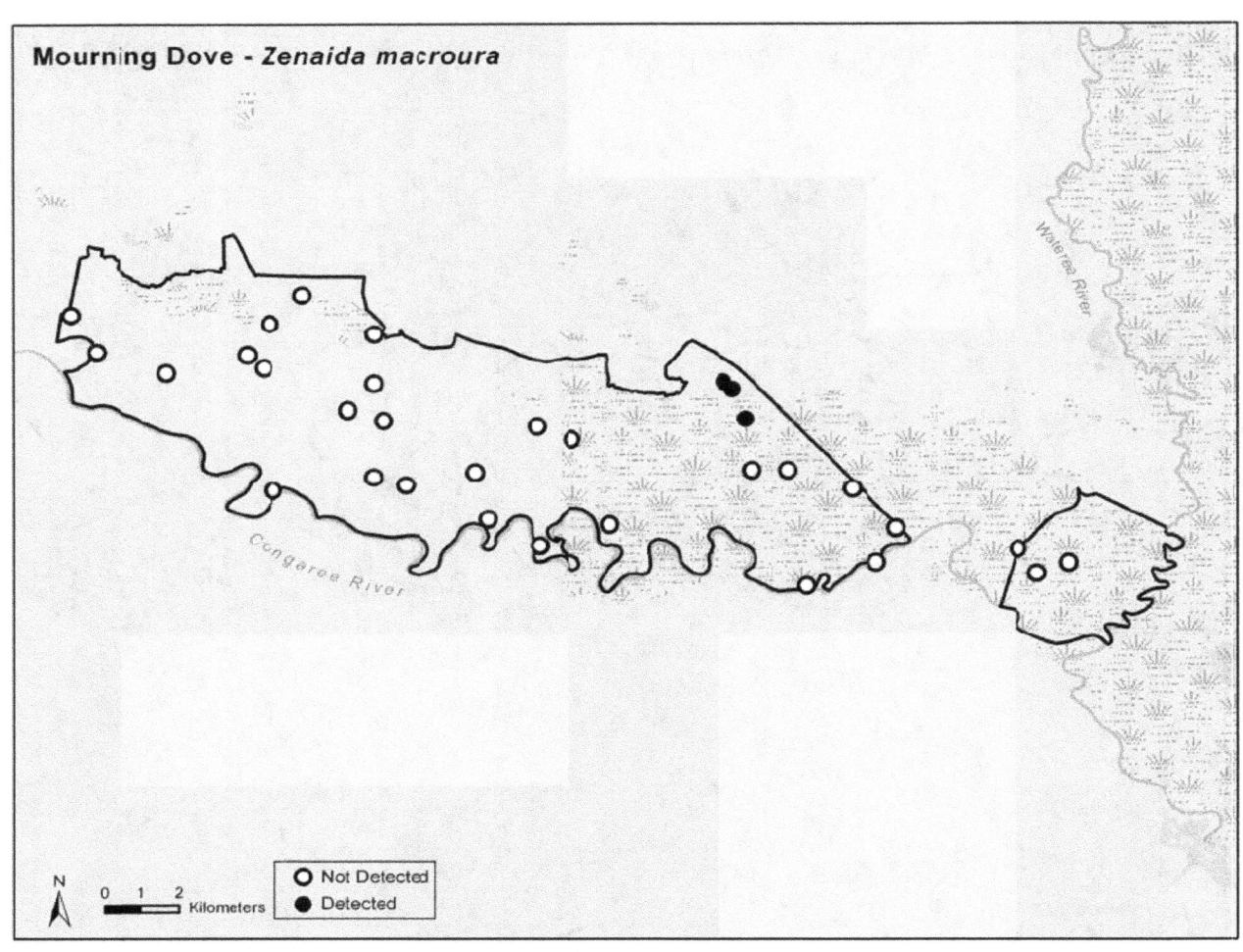

Figure D-37. Sampling locations where Mourning Dove (*Zenaida macroura*) was detected at CONG, 2009. ● = detected, ○ = not detected.

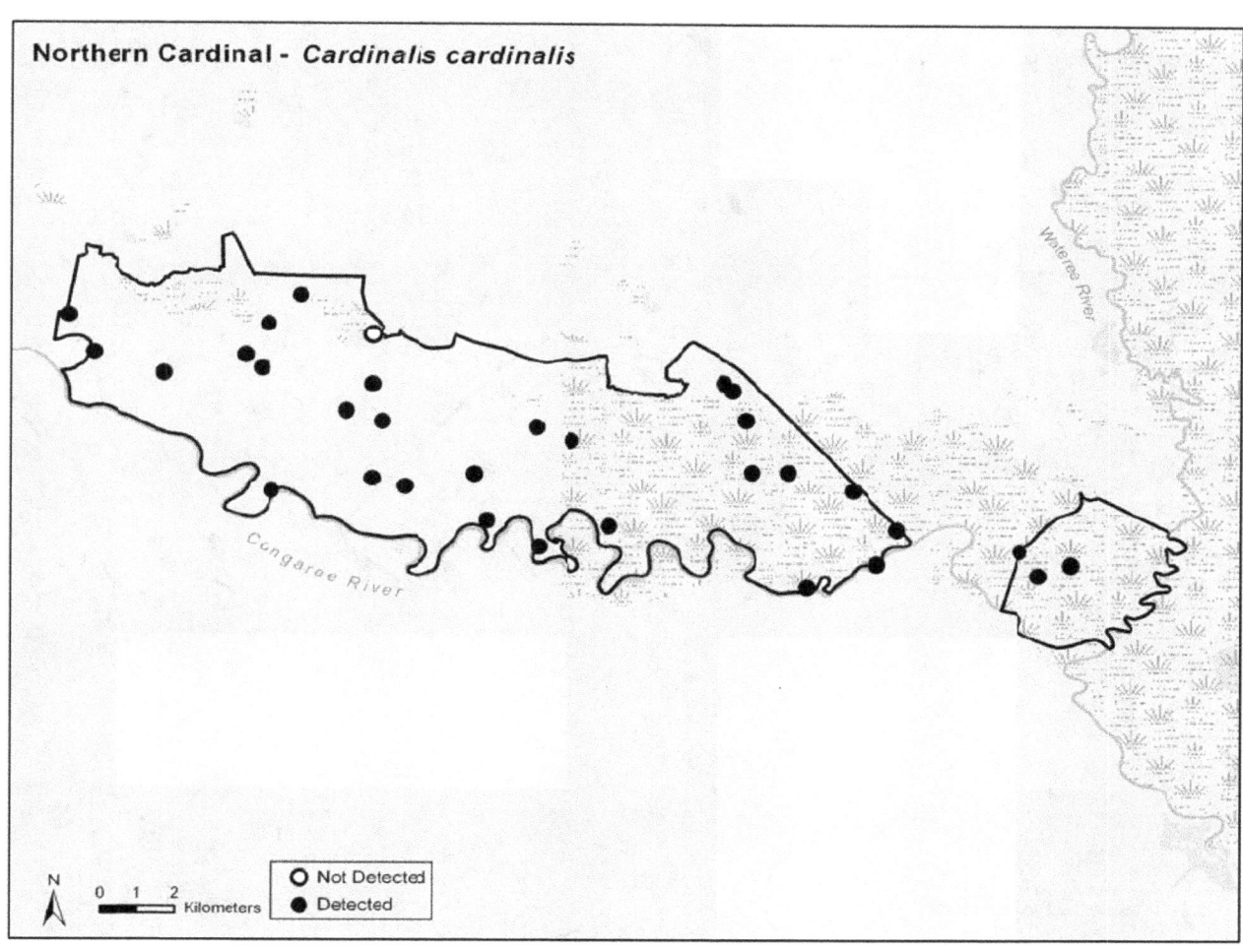

Figure D-38. Sampling locations where Northern Cardinal (:ardinalis cardinalis) was detected at CONG, 2009. ● = detected, ○ = not detected.

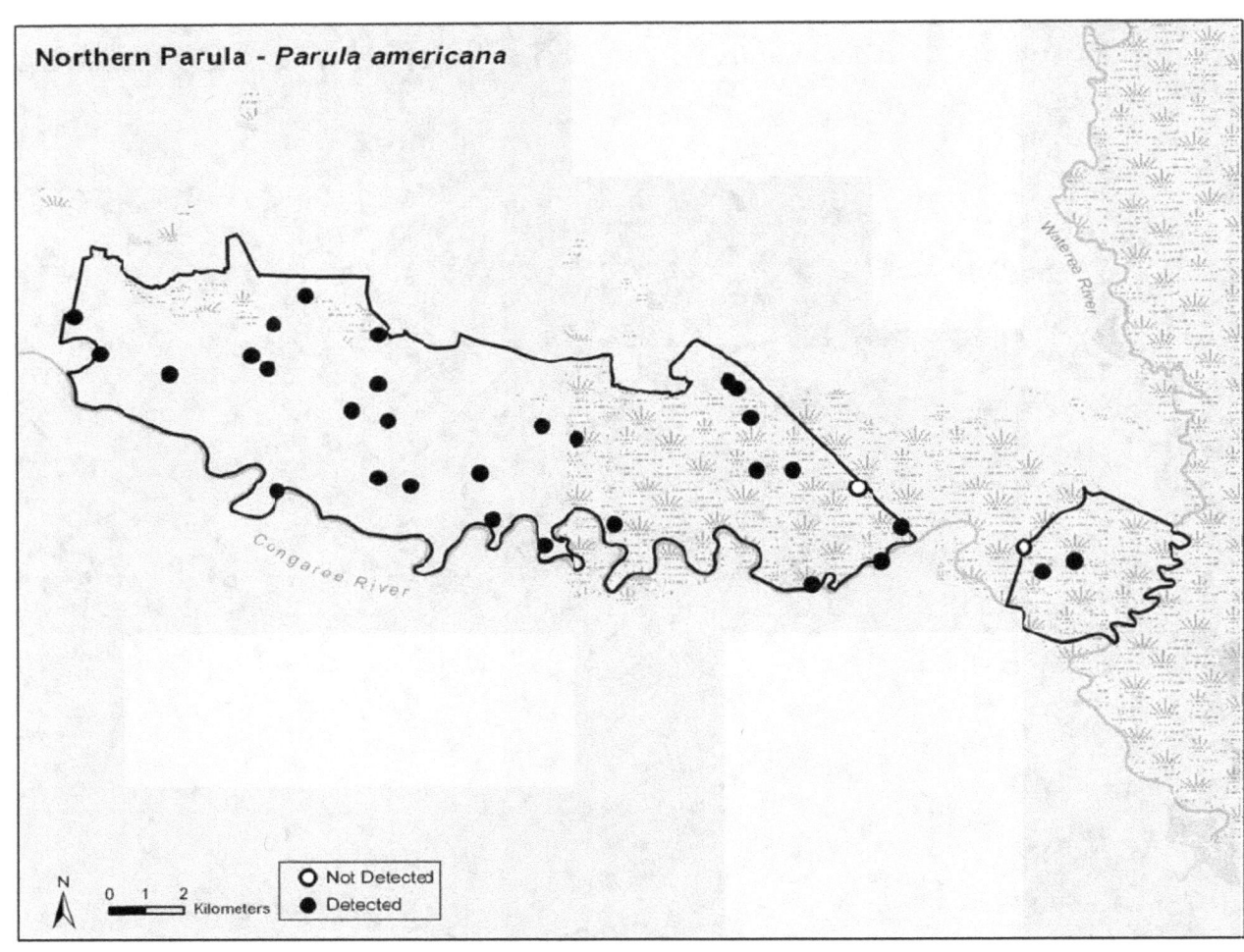

Figure D-39. Sampling locations where Northern Parula (*Parula americana*) was detected at CONG, 2009. ● = detected, ○ = not detected.

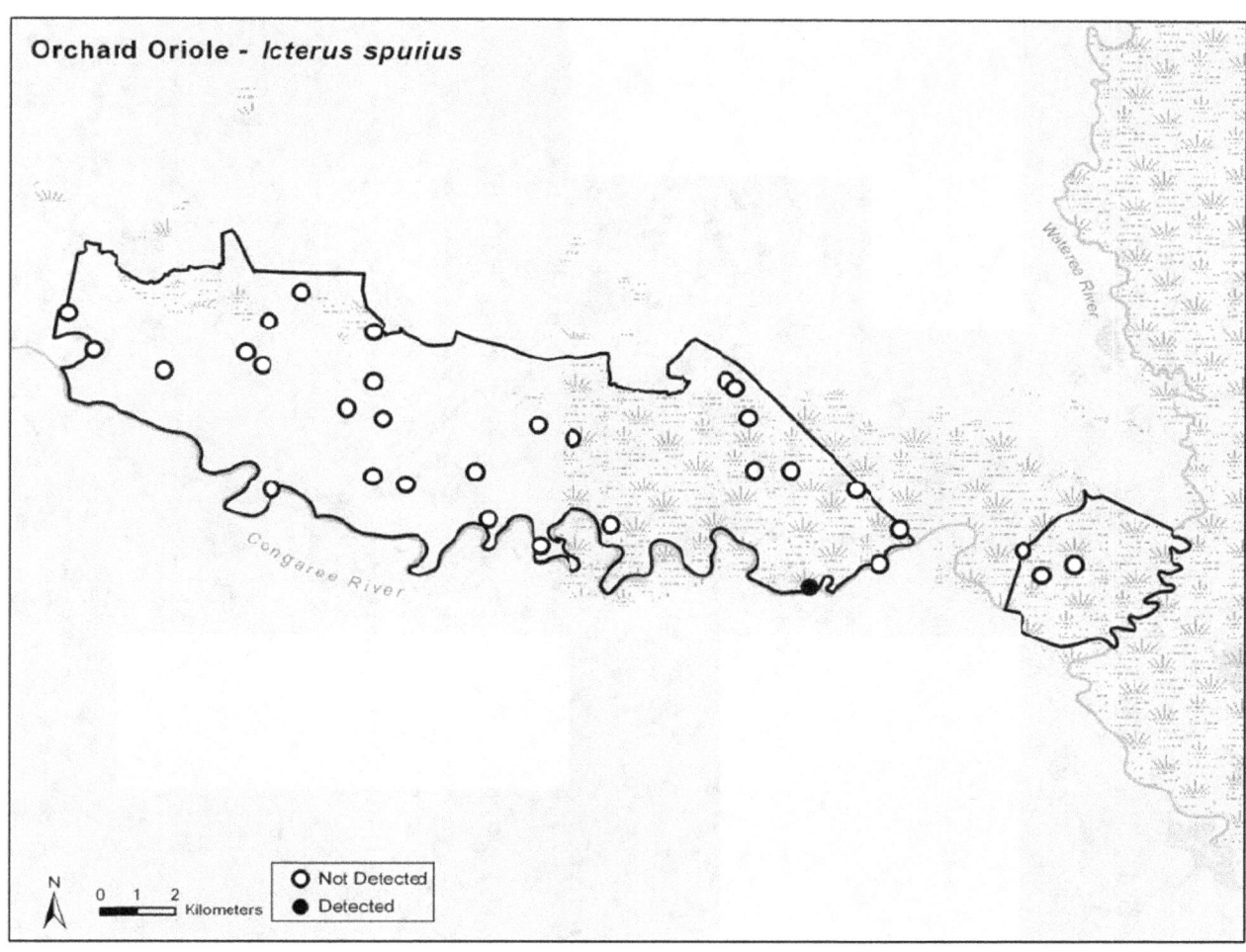

Figure D-40. Sampling locations where Orchard Oriole (*Icterus spurius*) was detected at CONG, 2009. ● = detected, ○ = not detected.

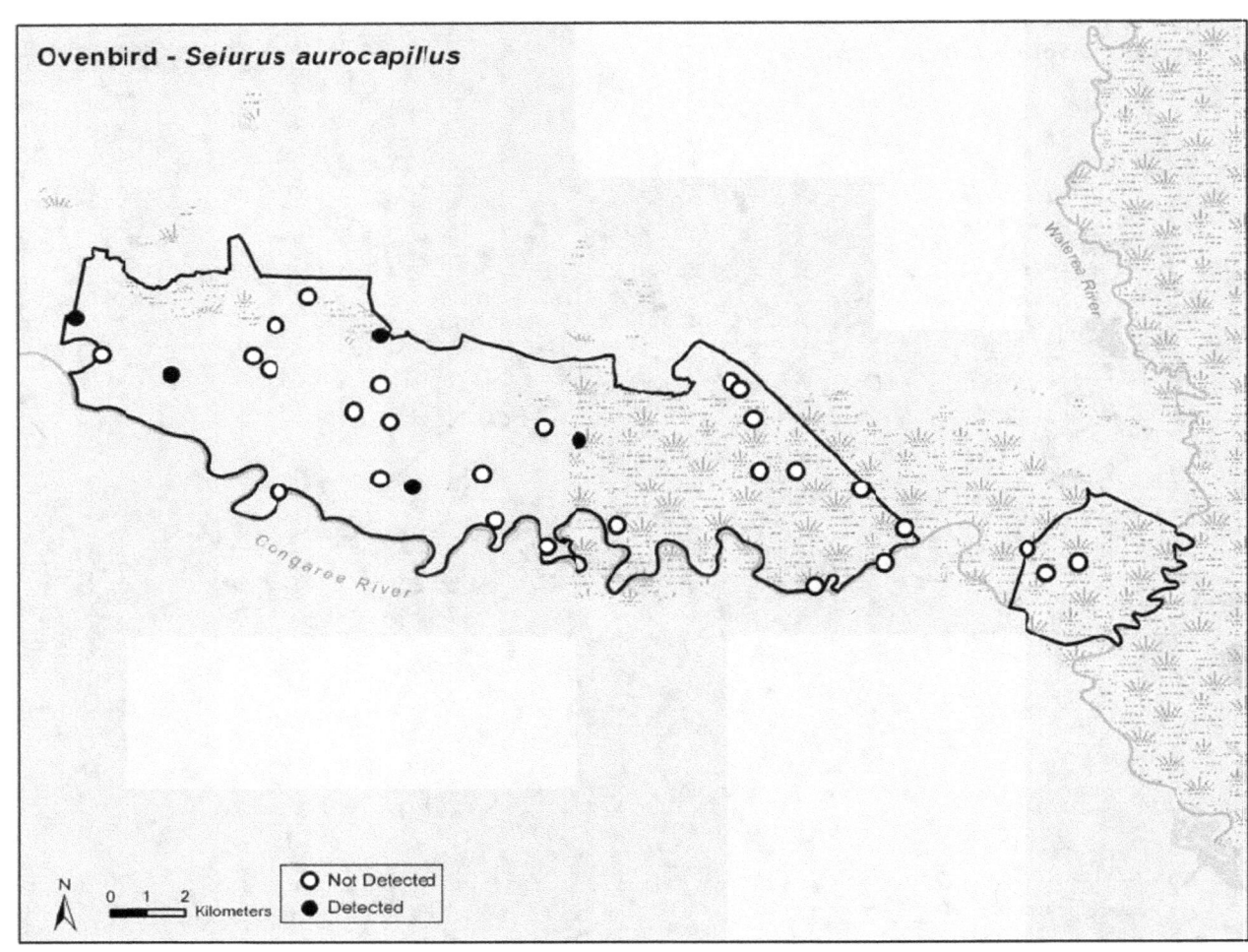

Figure D-41. Sampling locations where Ovenbird (*Seiurus aurocapillus*) was detected at CONG, 2009. ● = detected, ○ = not detected.

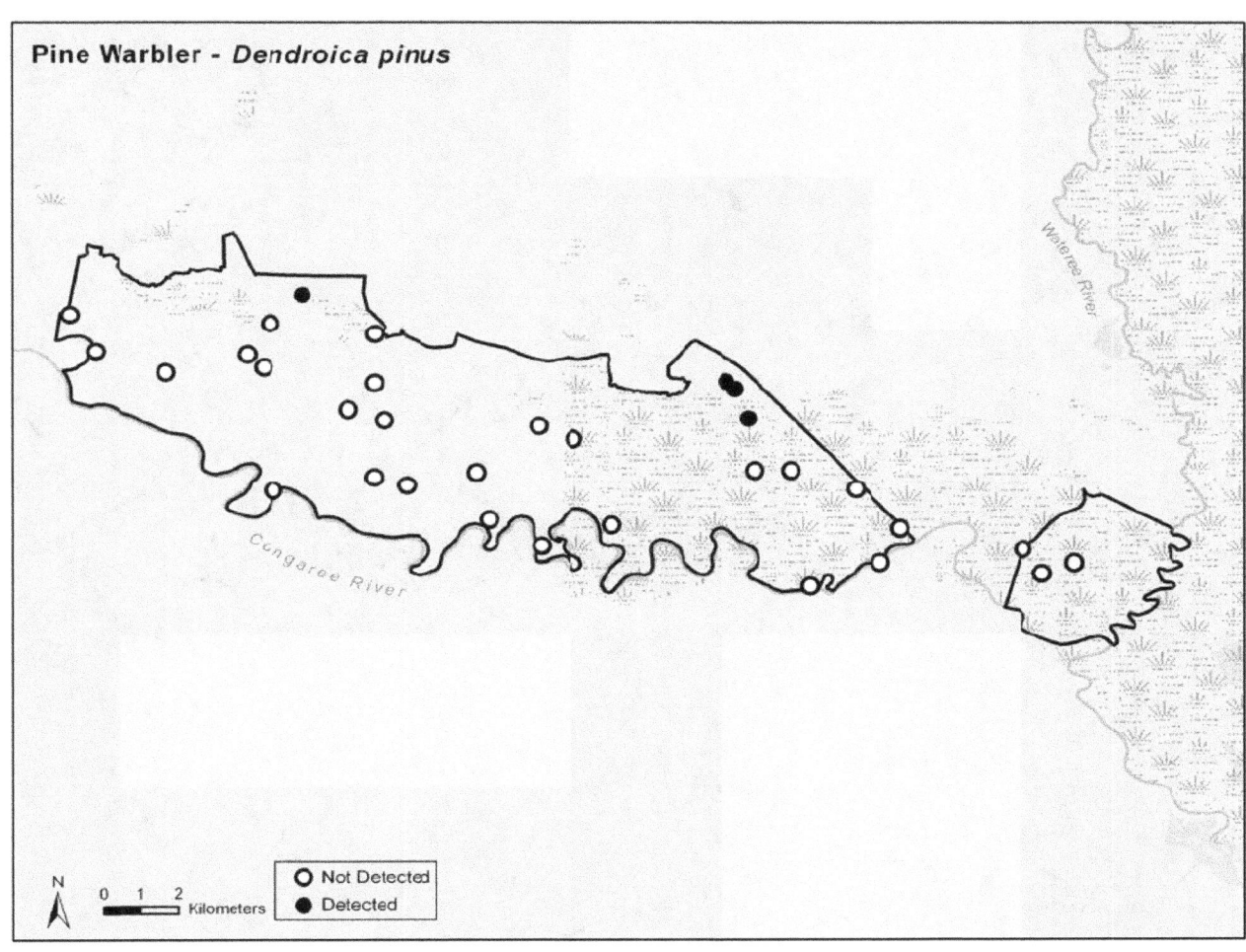

Figure D-42. Sampling locations where Pine Warbler (*Dend oica pinus*) was detected at CONG, 2009. ● = detected, ○ = not de:ected.

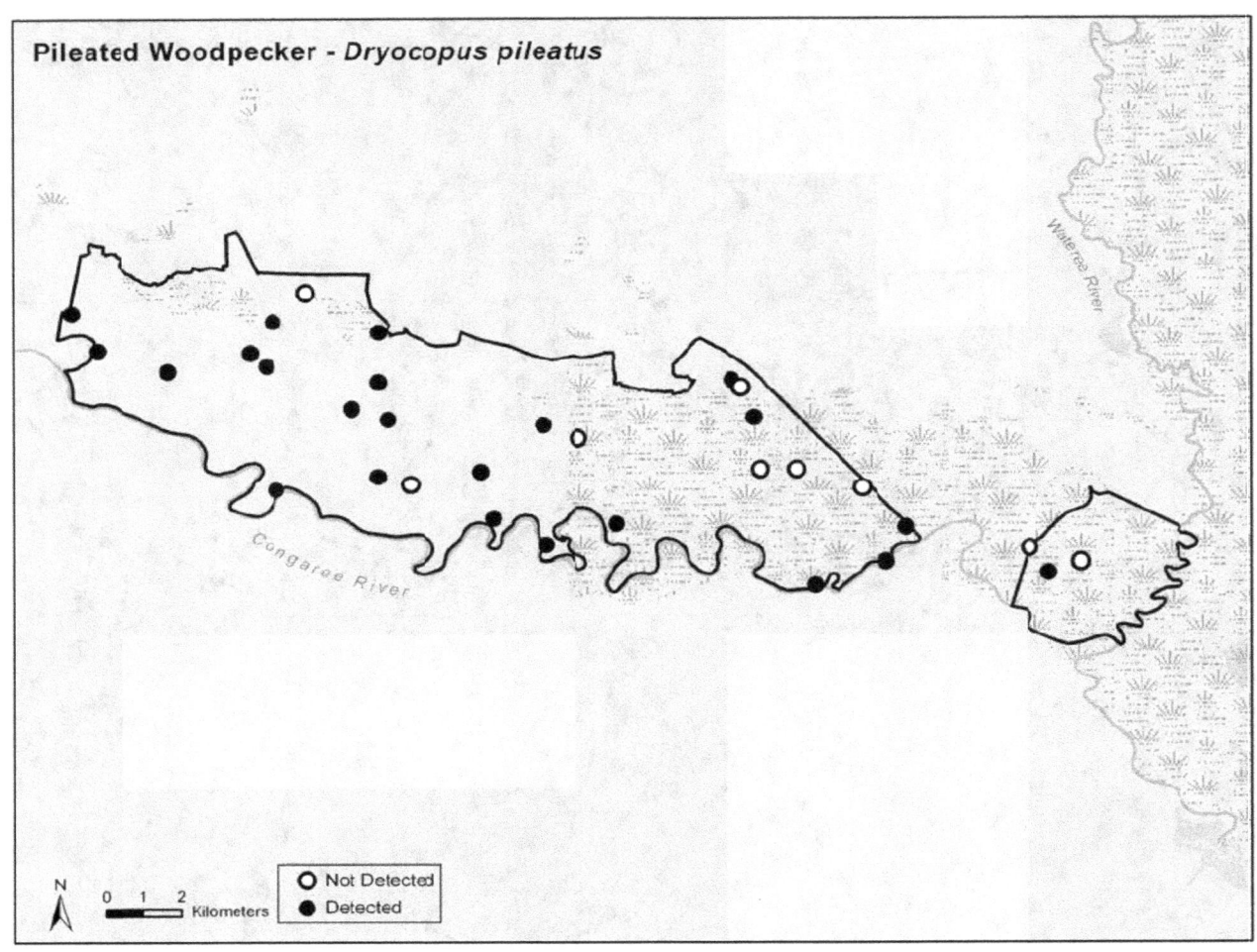

Figure D-43. Sampling locations where Pileated Woodpeck r (*Dryocopu ; pileatus*) was detected at CONG, 2009. ● = det cted, ○ = not detected.

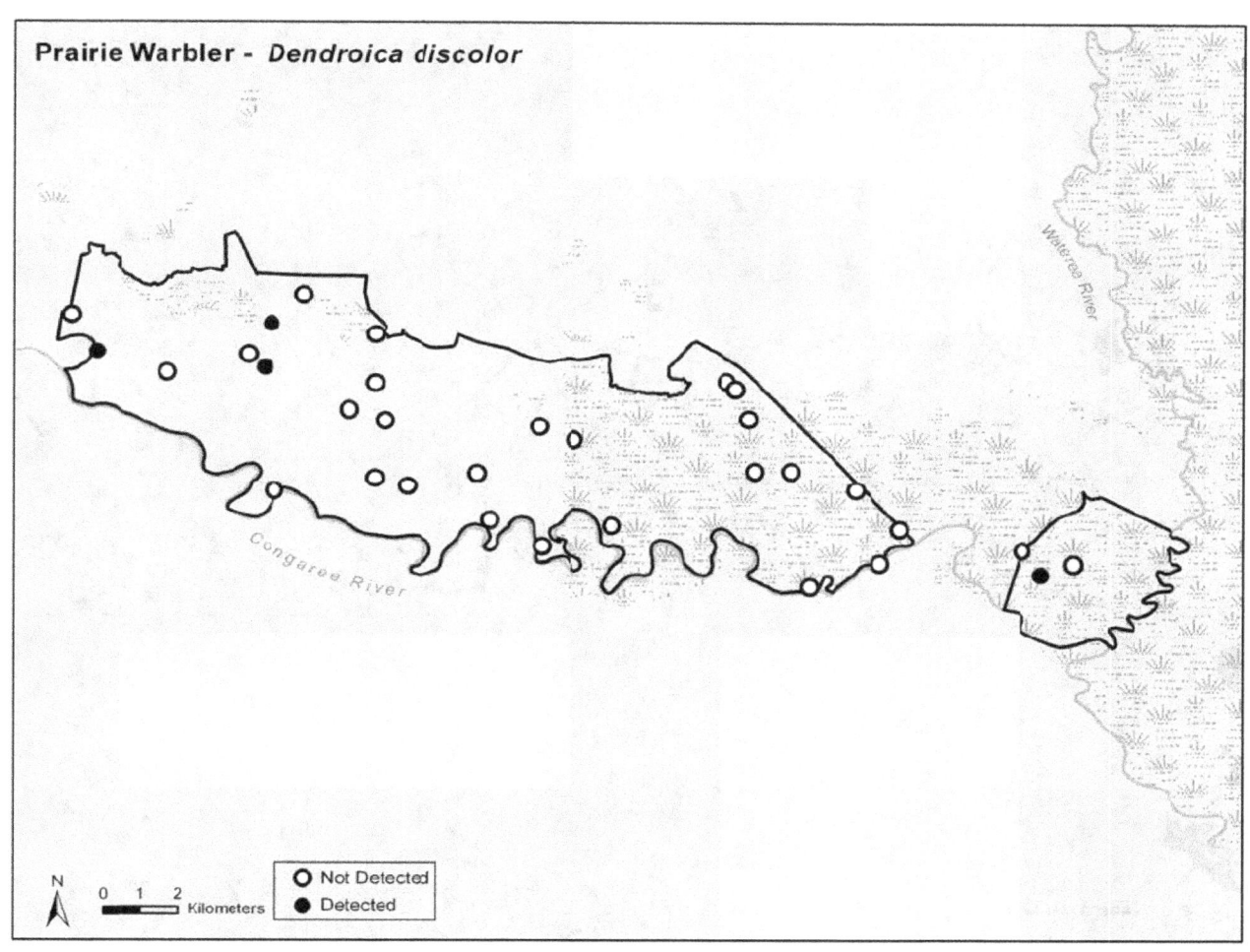

Figure D-44. Sampling locations where Prairie Warbler (*Dendroica discolor*) was detected at CONG, 2009. ● = detected, ○ = not detected.

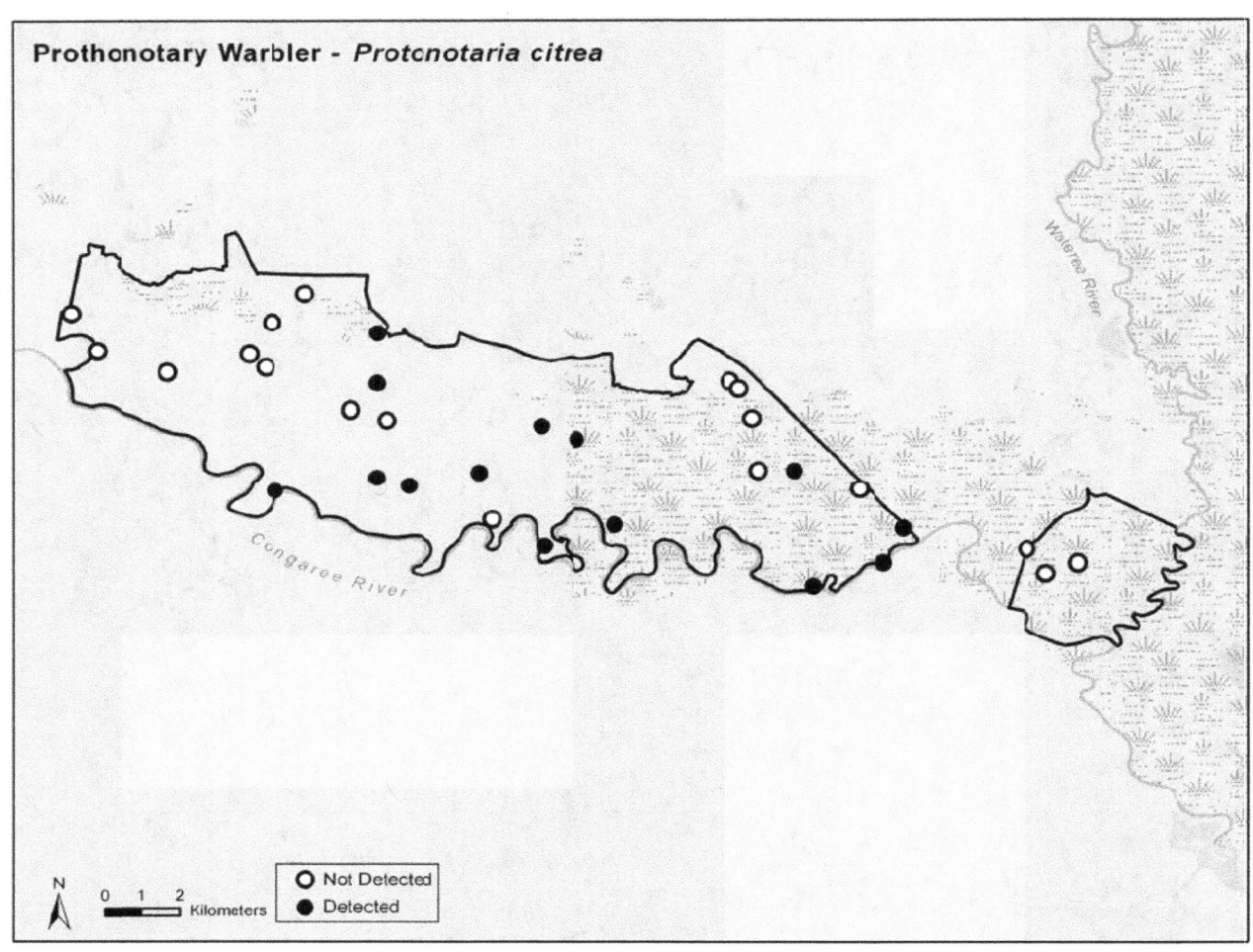

Figure D-45. Sampling locations where Prothonotary Warbler (*Protonota ia citrea*) was detected at CONG, 2009. ● = det cted, ○ = not detected.

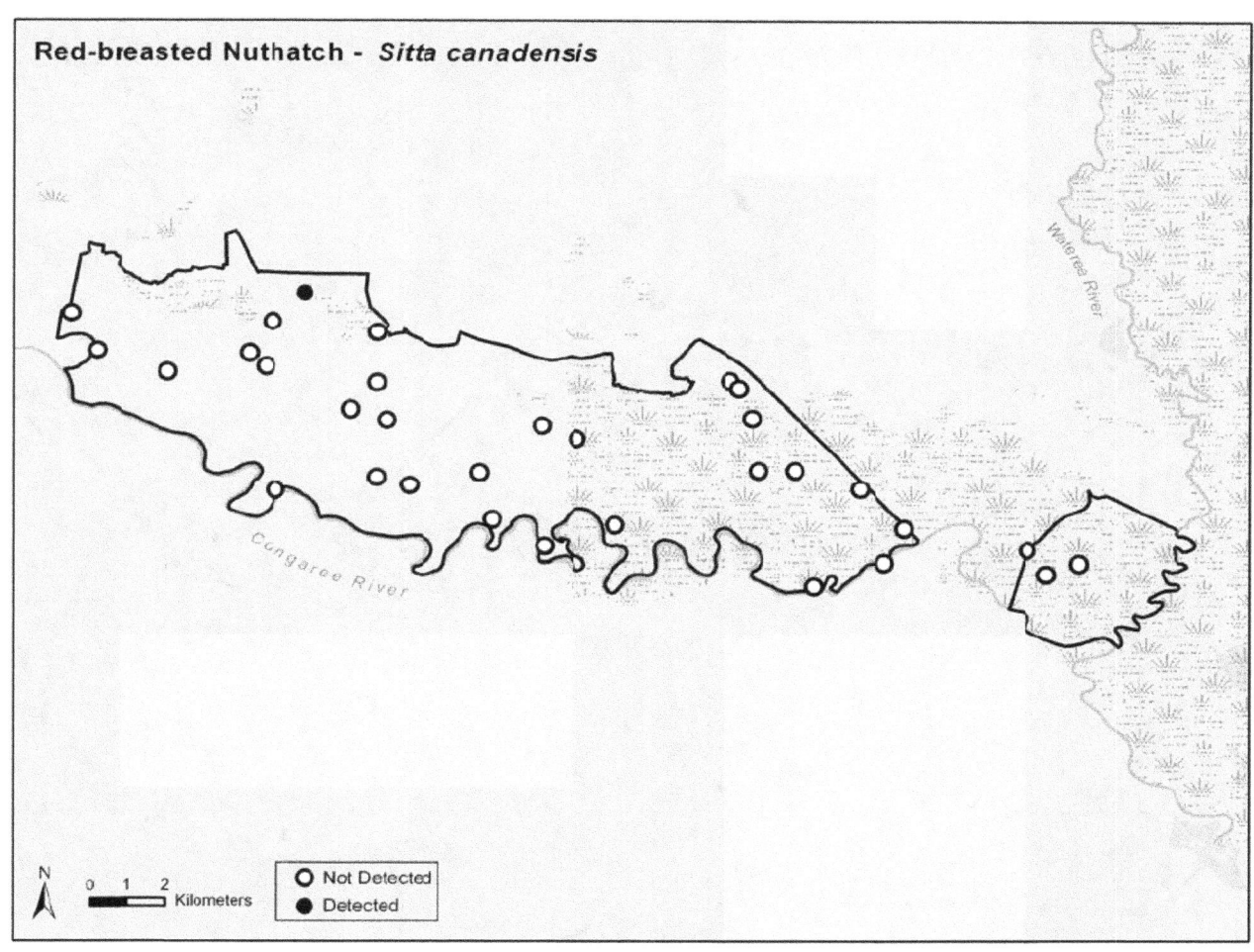

Figure D-46. Sampling locations where Red-breasted Nuthatch (*Sitta ca ɪadensis*) was detected at CONG, 2009. ● = det cted, ○ = not detected.

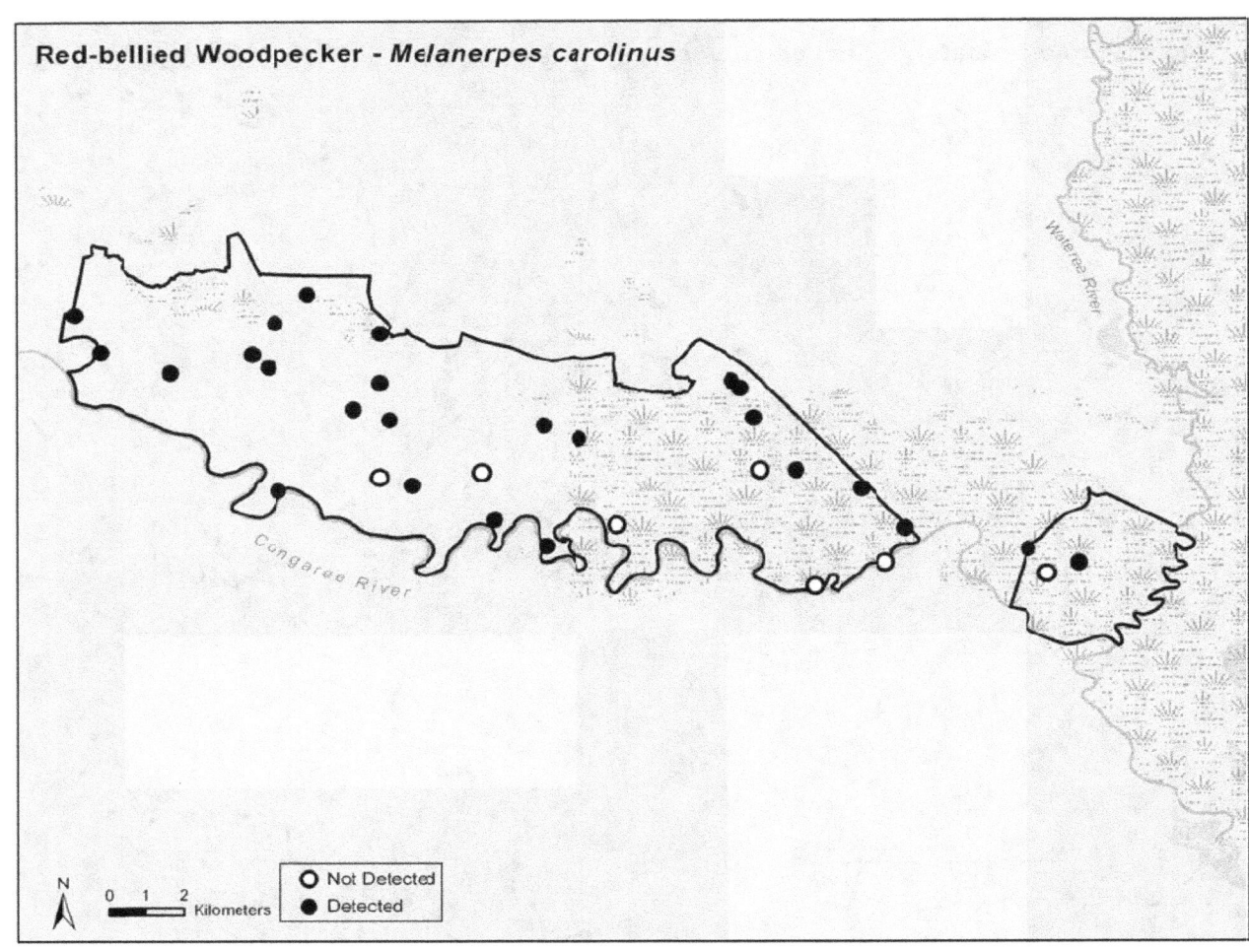

Figure D-47. Sampling locations where Red-bellied Woodpecker (*Melan rpes carolinus*) was detected at CONG, 2009. ● = det cted, ○ = not detected.

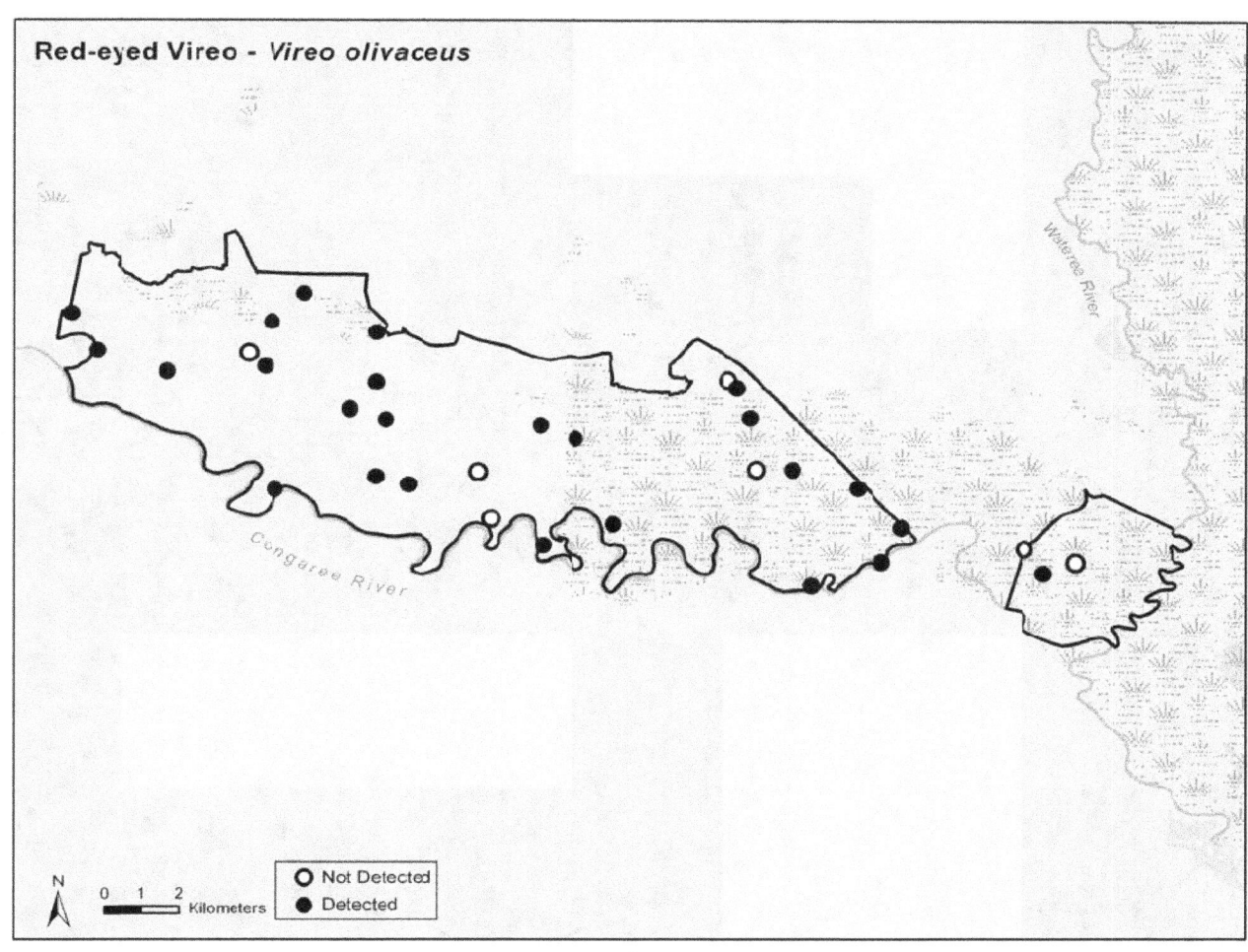

Figure D-48. Sampling locations where Red-eyed Vireo (*Vireo olivaceus*) was detected at CONG, 2009.
● = detected, ○ = not detected.

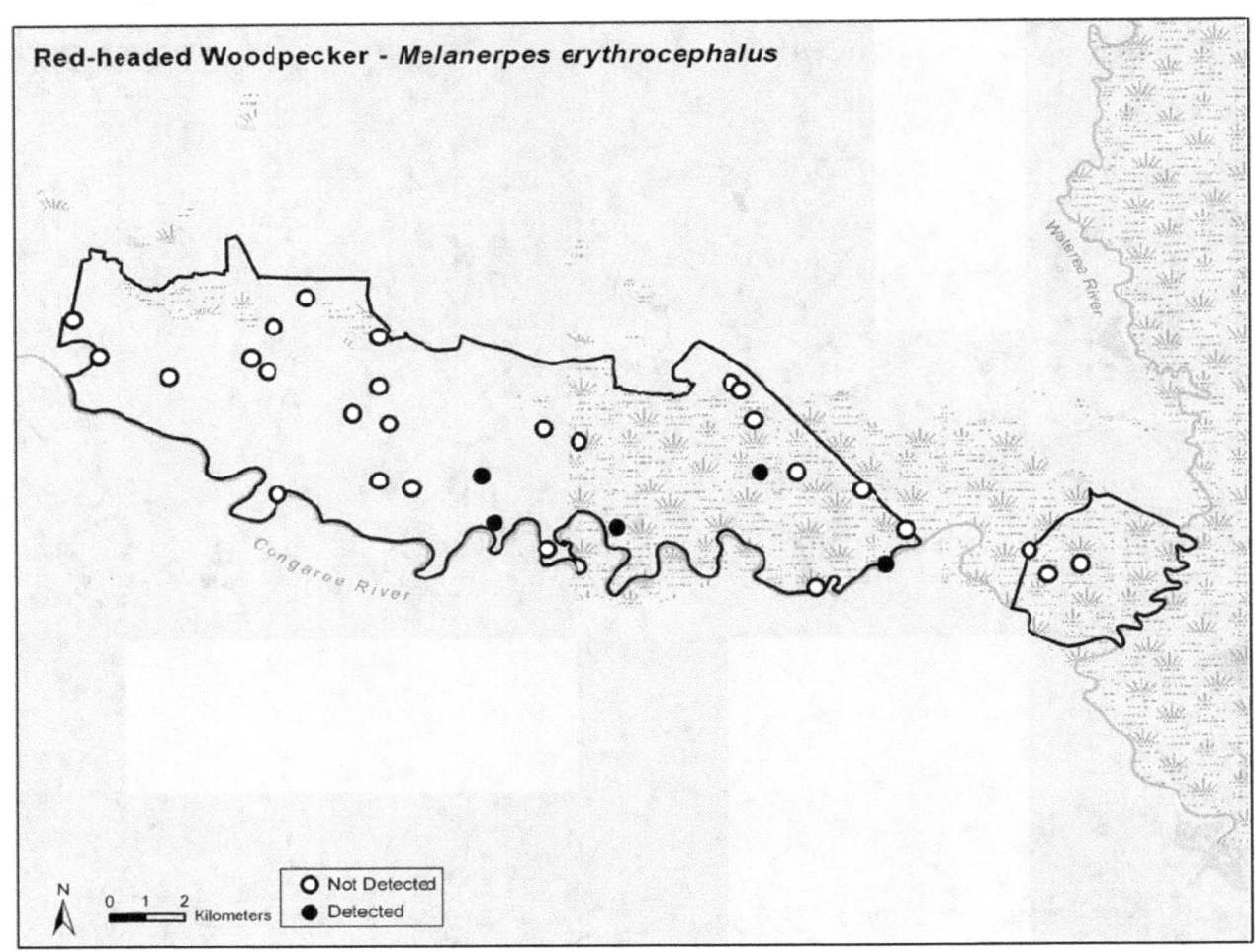

Figure D-49. Sampling locations where Red-headed Woodpecker (*Melanerpes erythrocephalus*) was detected at CONG, 2009. ● = detected, ○ = not detected.

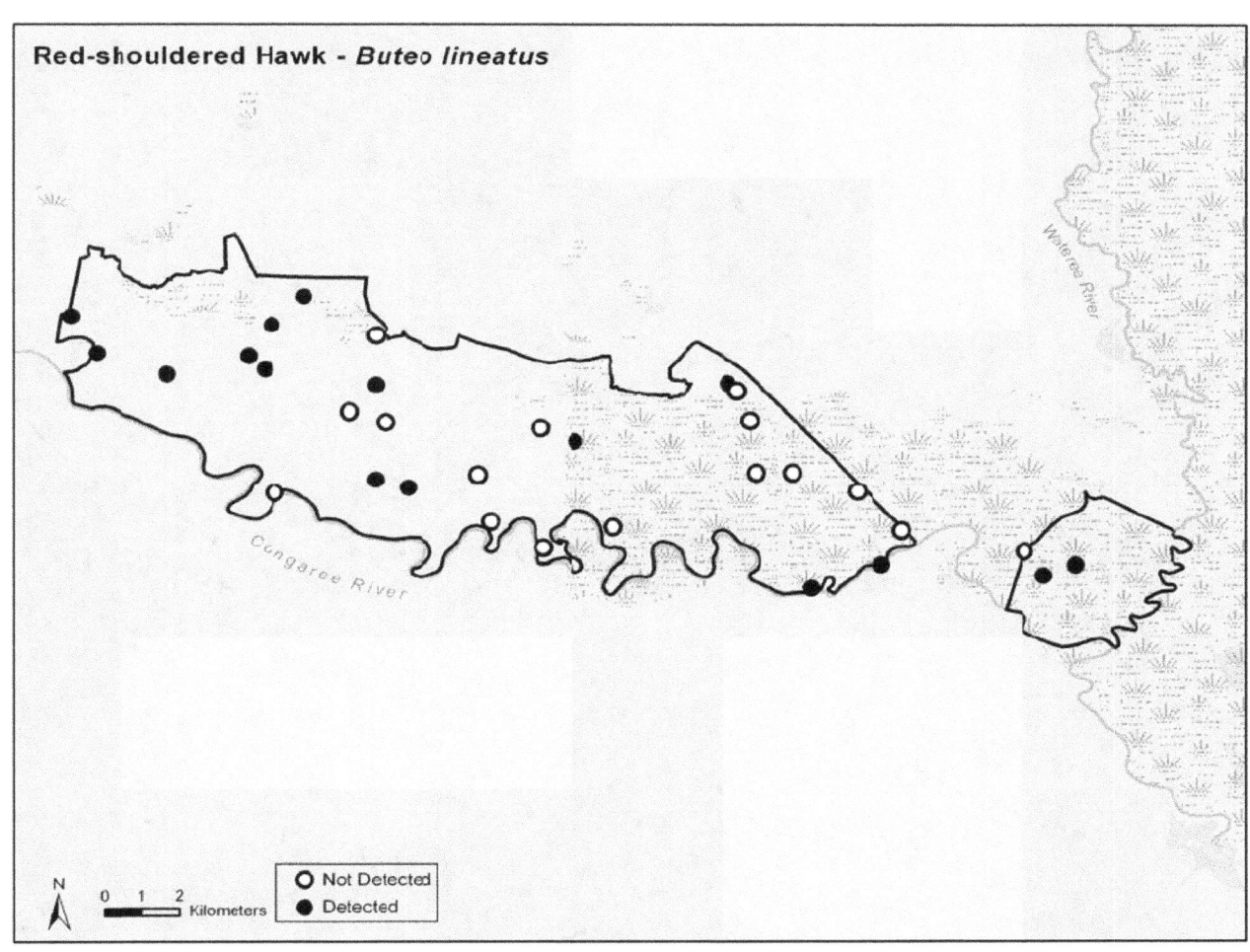

Figure D-50. Sampling locations where Red-shouldered Hawk (*Buteo lineatus*) was detected at CONG, 2009. ● = detected, ○ = not detected.

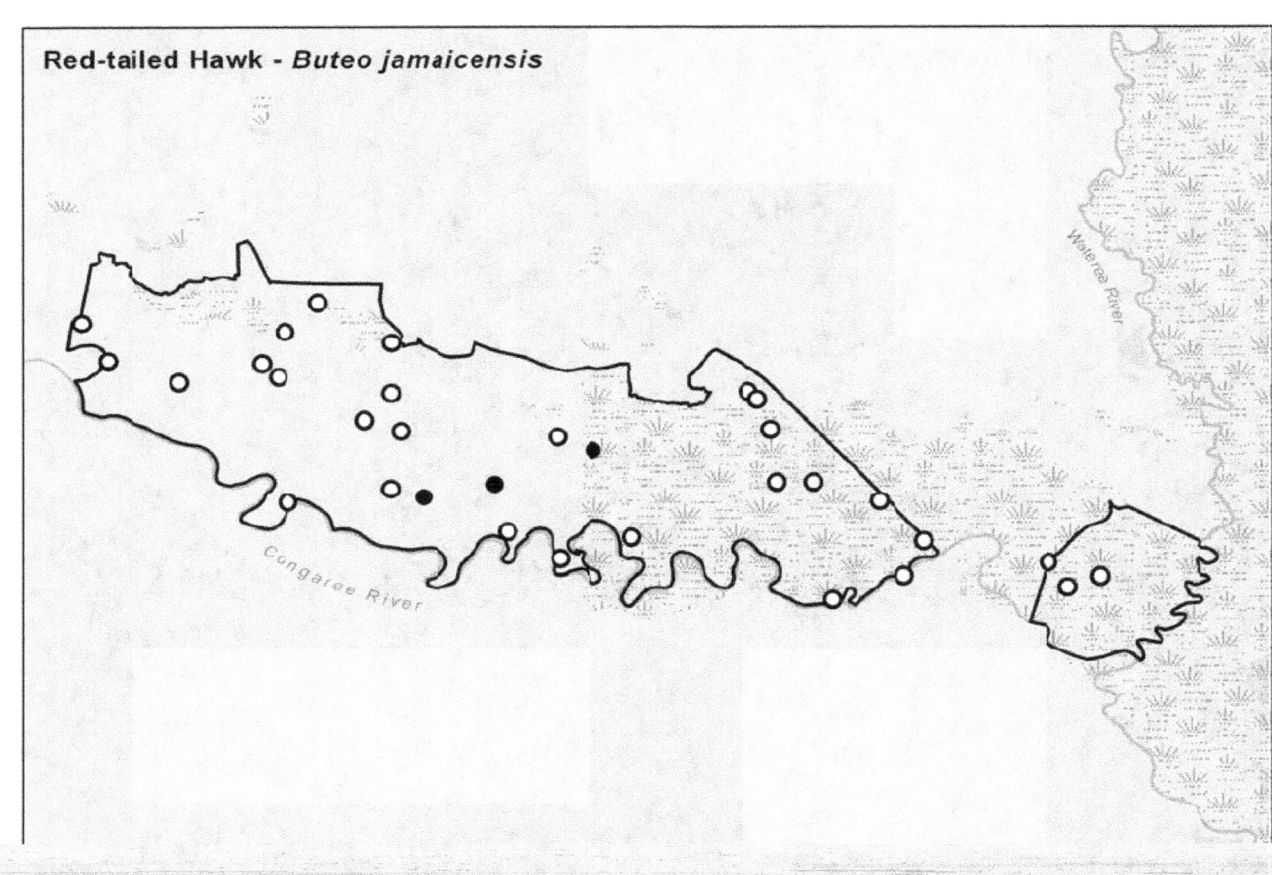

Red-tailed Hawk - *Buteo jamaicensis*

tailed Hawk (*Buteo jamaicensis*) was detected at CONG,

Figure D-51. Sampling locations where 2009. ● = detected, ○ = not detected.

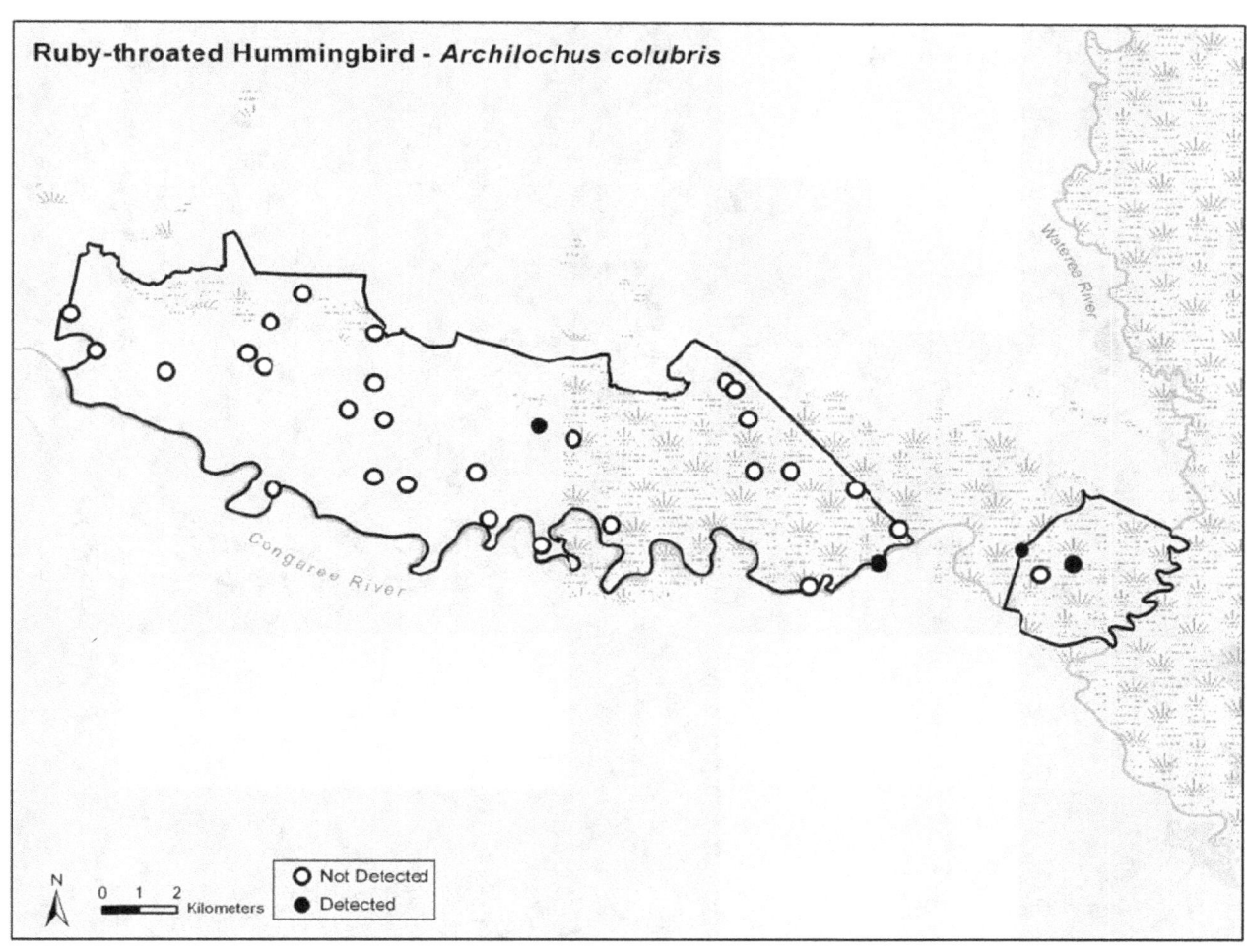

Figure D-52. Sampling locations where Ruby-throated Hum ningbird (*Archilochus colubris*) was detected at CONG, 2009. ● = detected, ○ = not detected.

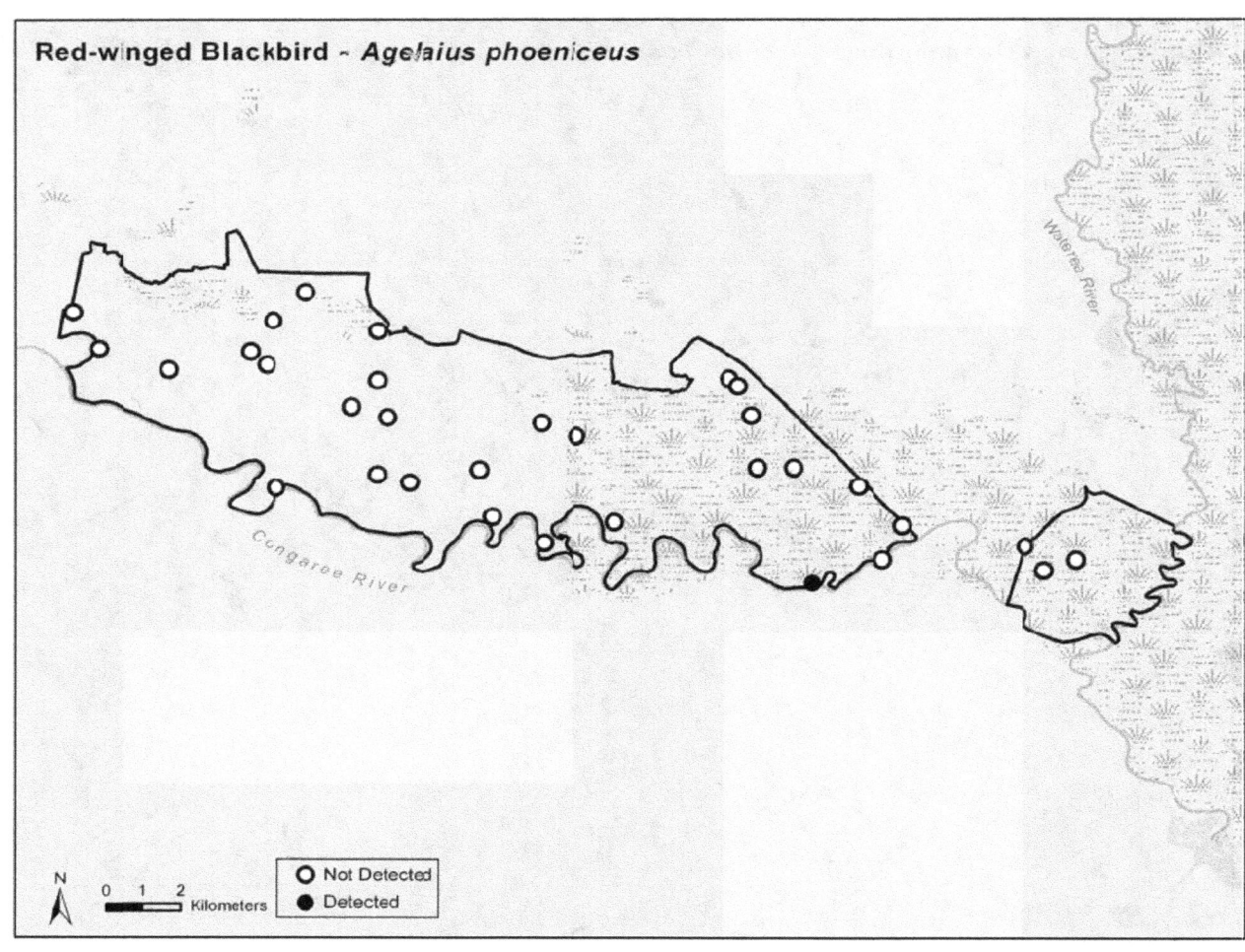

Figure D-53. Sampling locations where Red-winged Blackbird (*Agelaius phoeniceus*) was detected at CONG, 2009. ● = det cted, ○ = not detected.

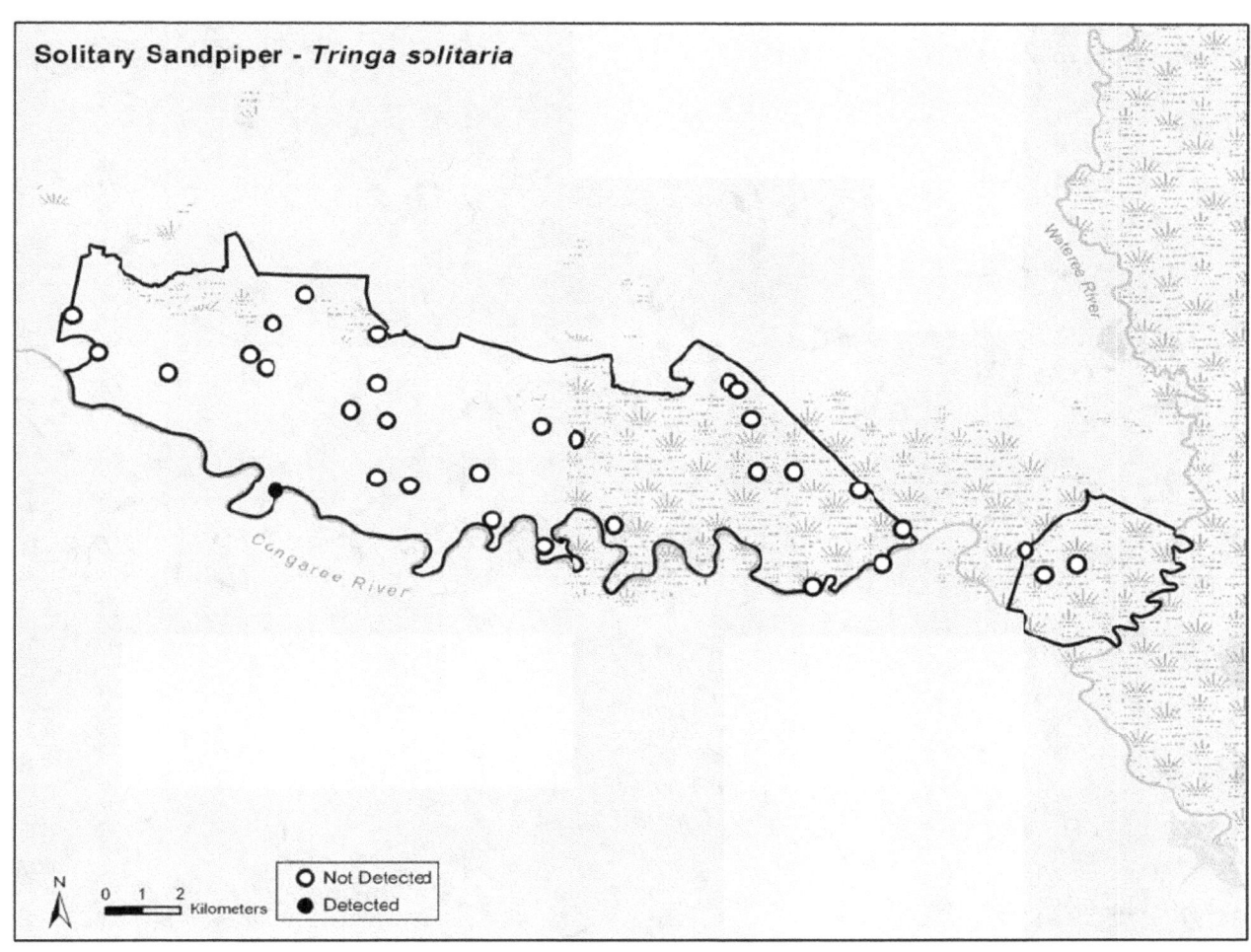

Figure D-54. Sampling locations where Solitary Sandpiper (*Tringa solitaria*) was detected at CONG, 2009. ● = detected, ○ = not detected.

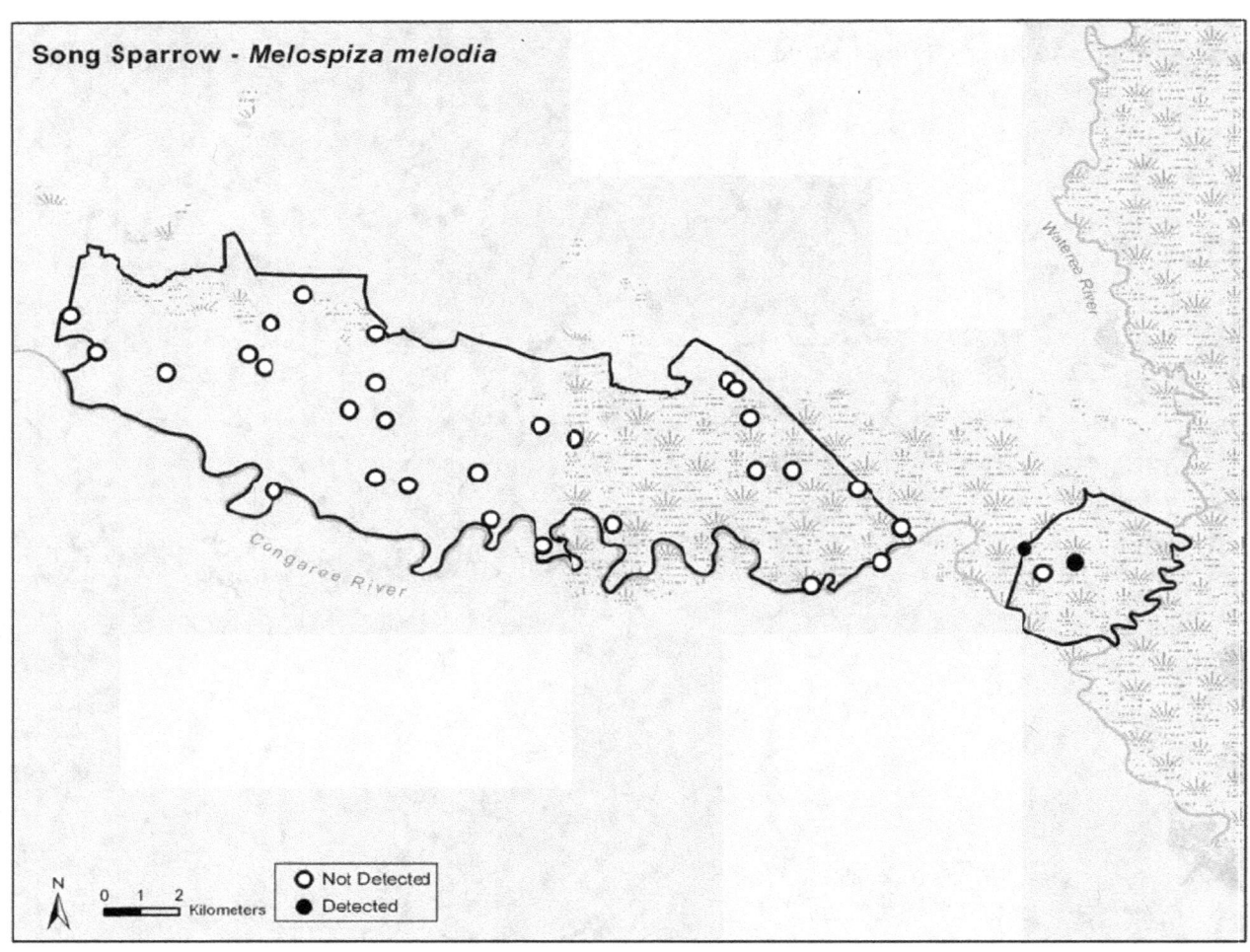

Figure D-55. Sampling locations where Song Sparrow (*Melospiza melodia*) was detected at CONG, 2009. ● = detected, ○ = not detected.

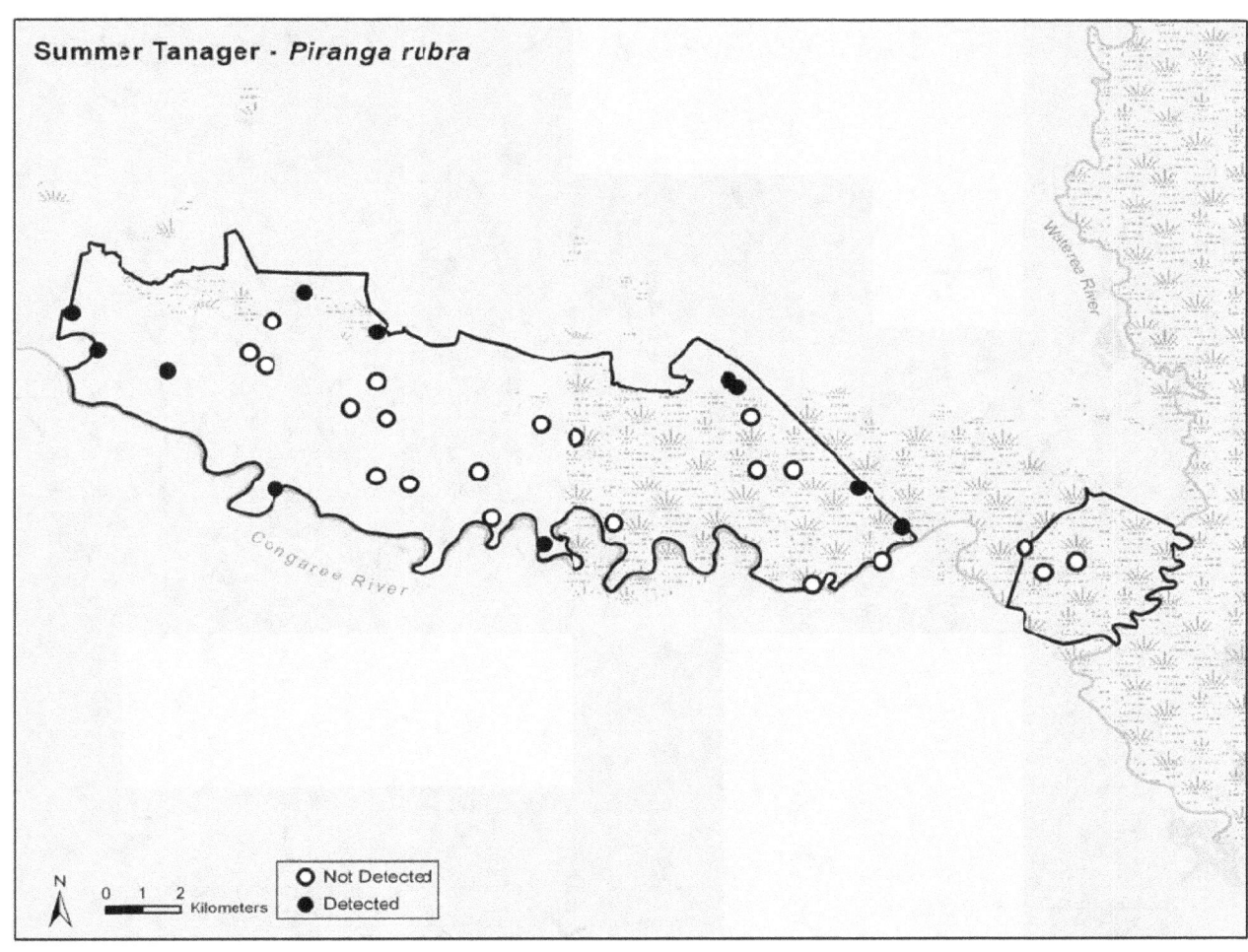

Figure D-56. Sampling locations where Summer Tanager (*Piranga rubra*) was detected at CONG, 2009. ● = detected, ○ = not detected.

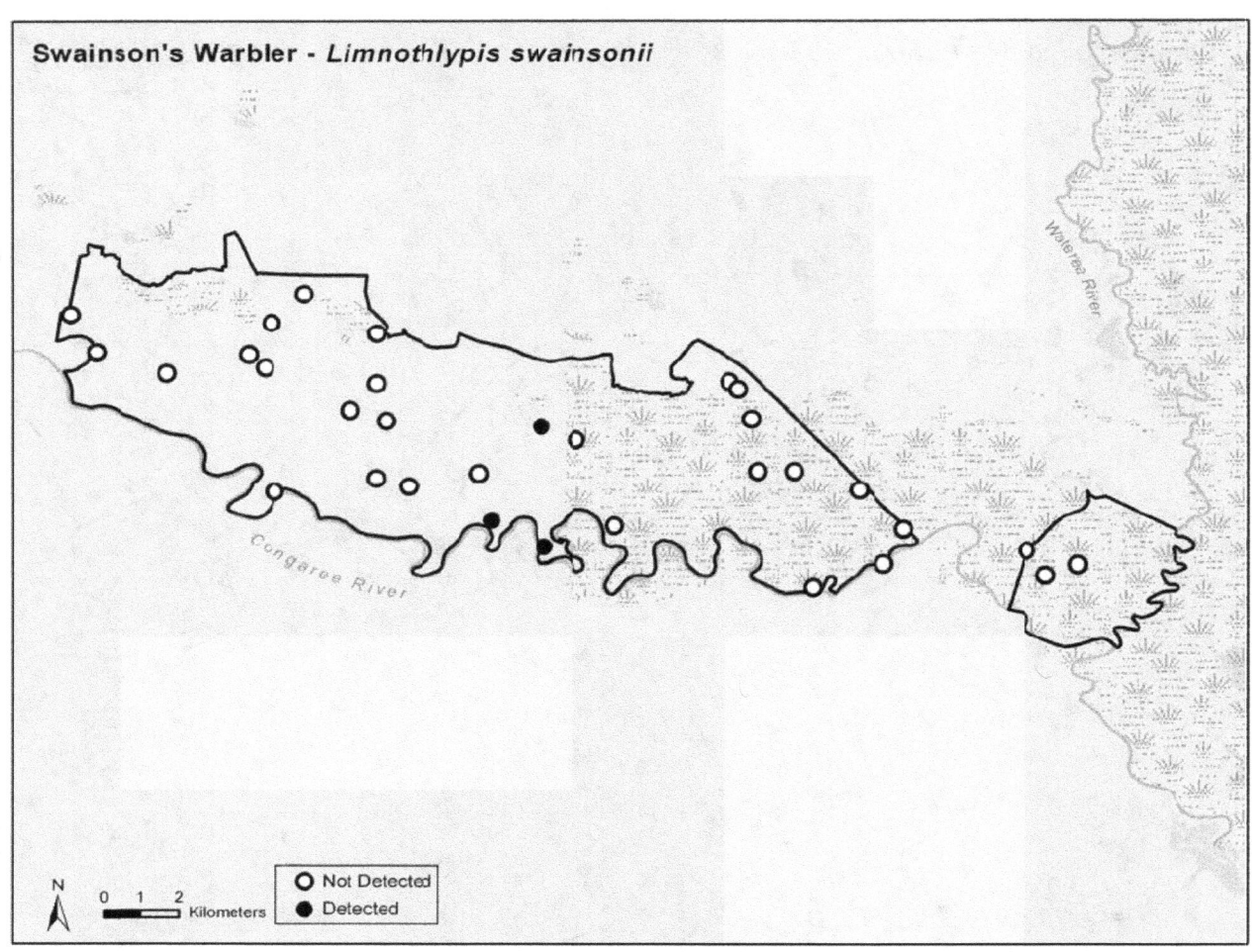

Figure D-57. Sampling locations where Swainson's Warbler (*Limnothlypi s swainsonii*) was detected at CONG, 2009. ● = det cted, ○ = not detected.

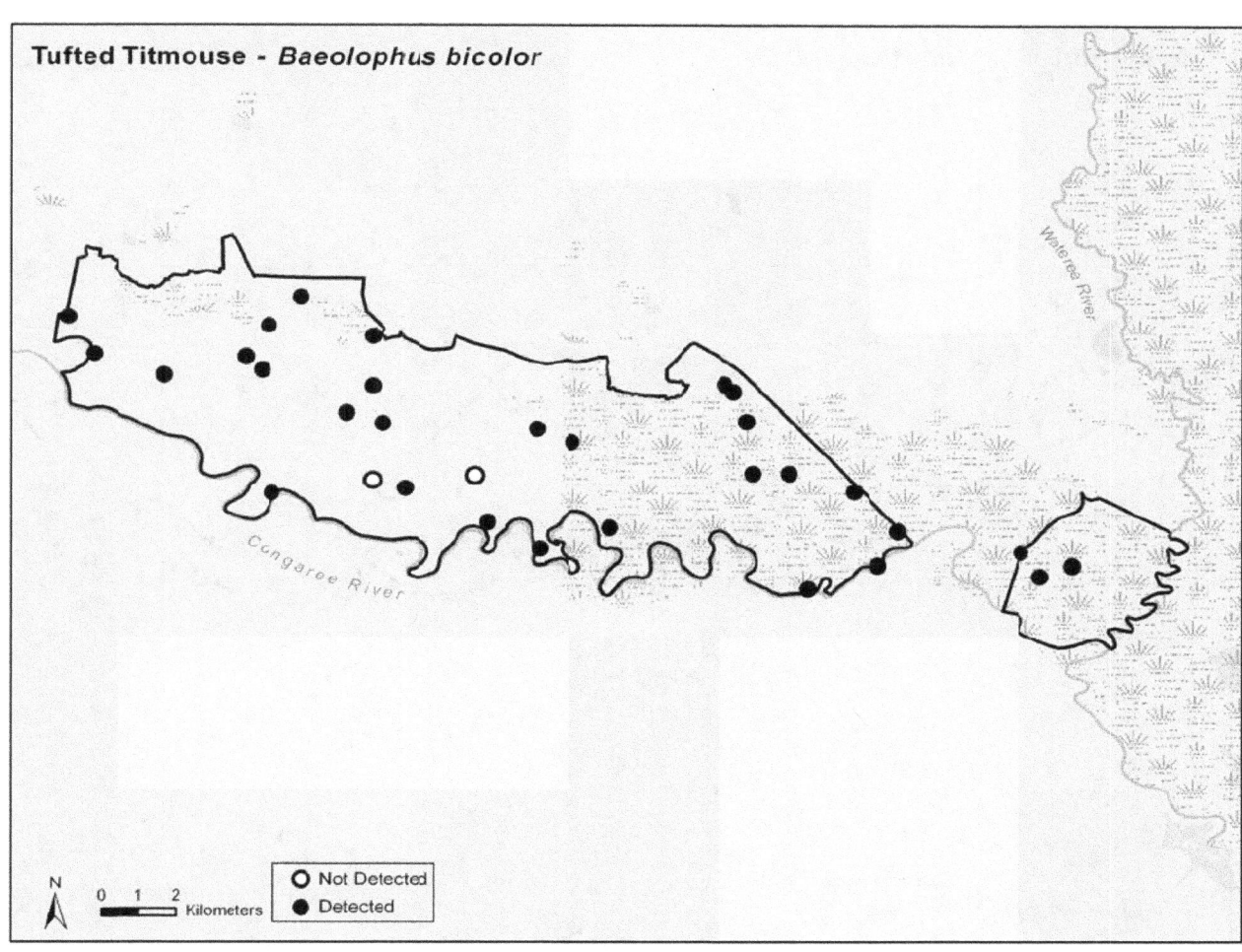

Figure D-58. Sampling locations where Tufted Titmouse (*Baeolophus bicolor*) was detected at CONG, 2009. ● = detected, ○ = not detected.

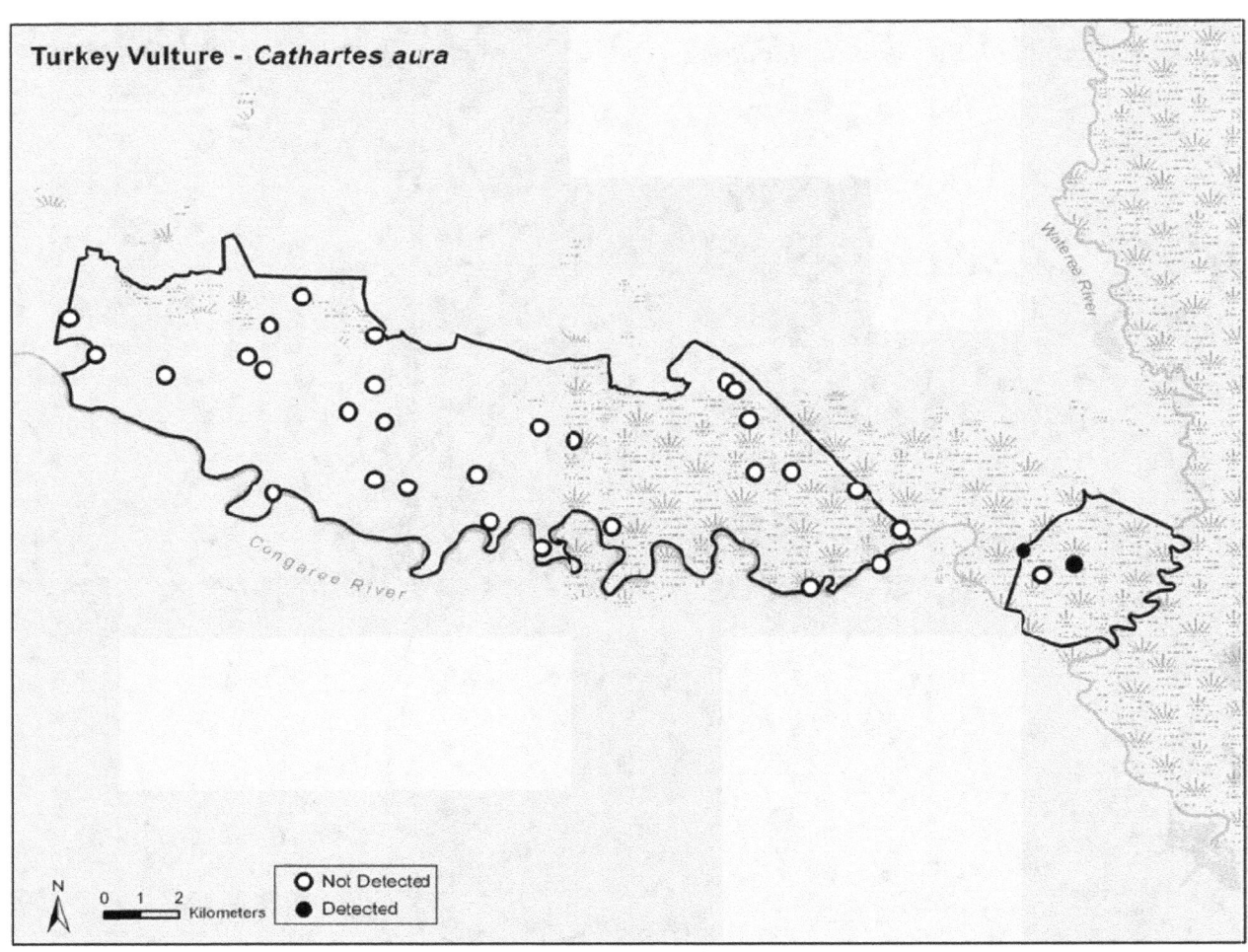

Figure D-59. Sampling locations where Turkey Vulture (*Cathartes aura*) was detected at CONG, 2009. ● = detected, ○ = not detected.

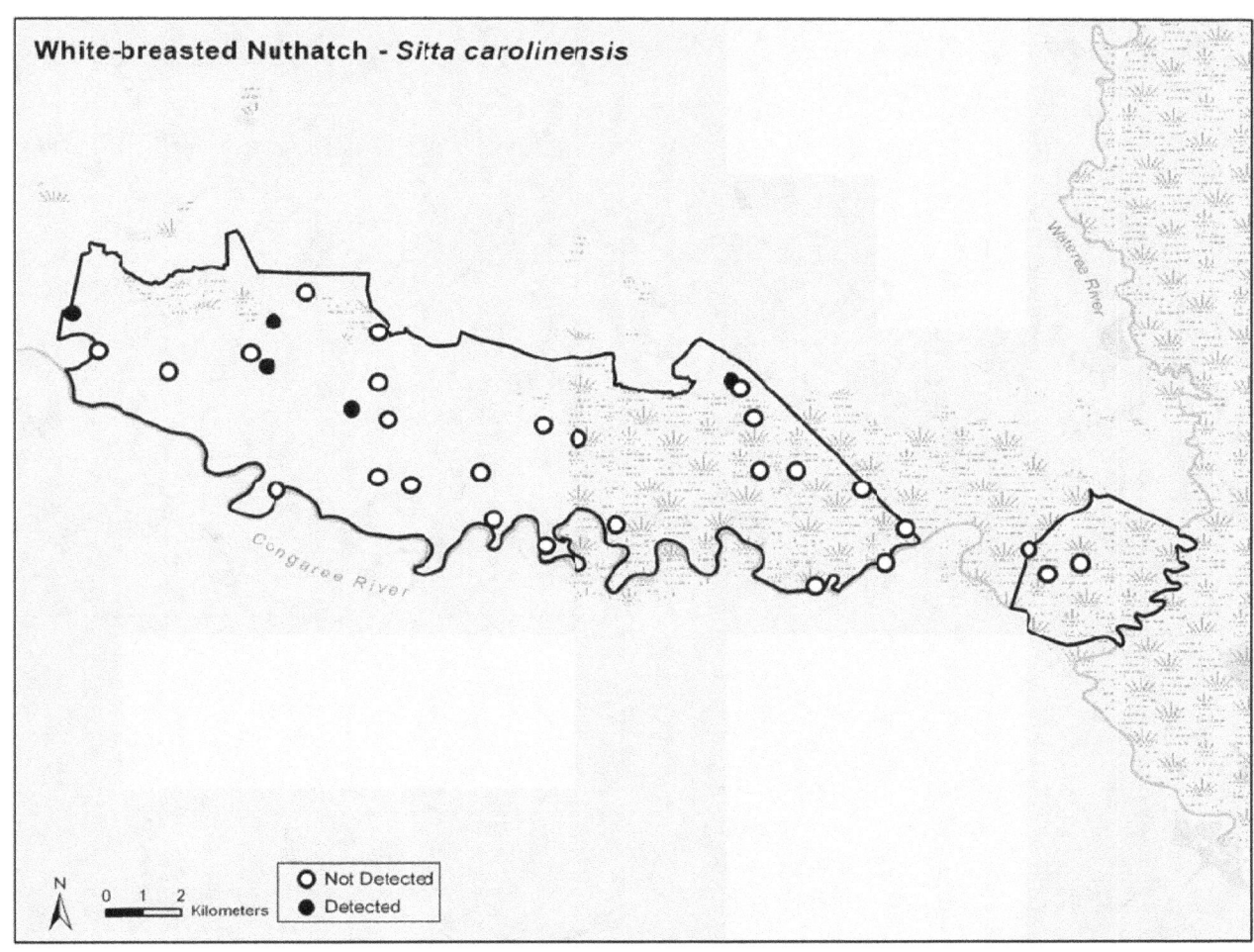

Figure D-60. Sampling locations where White-breasted Nut atch (*Sitta c arolinensis*) was detected at CONG, 2009. ● = det cted, ○ = not detected.

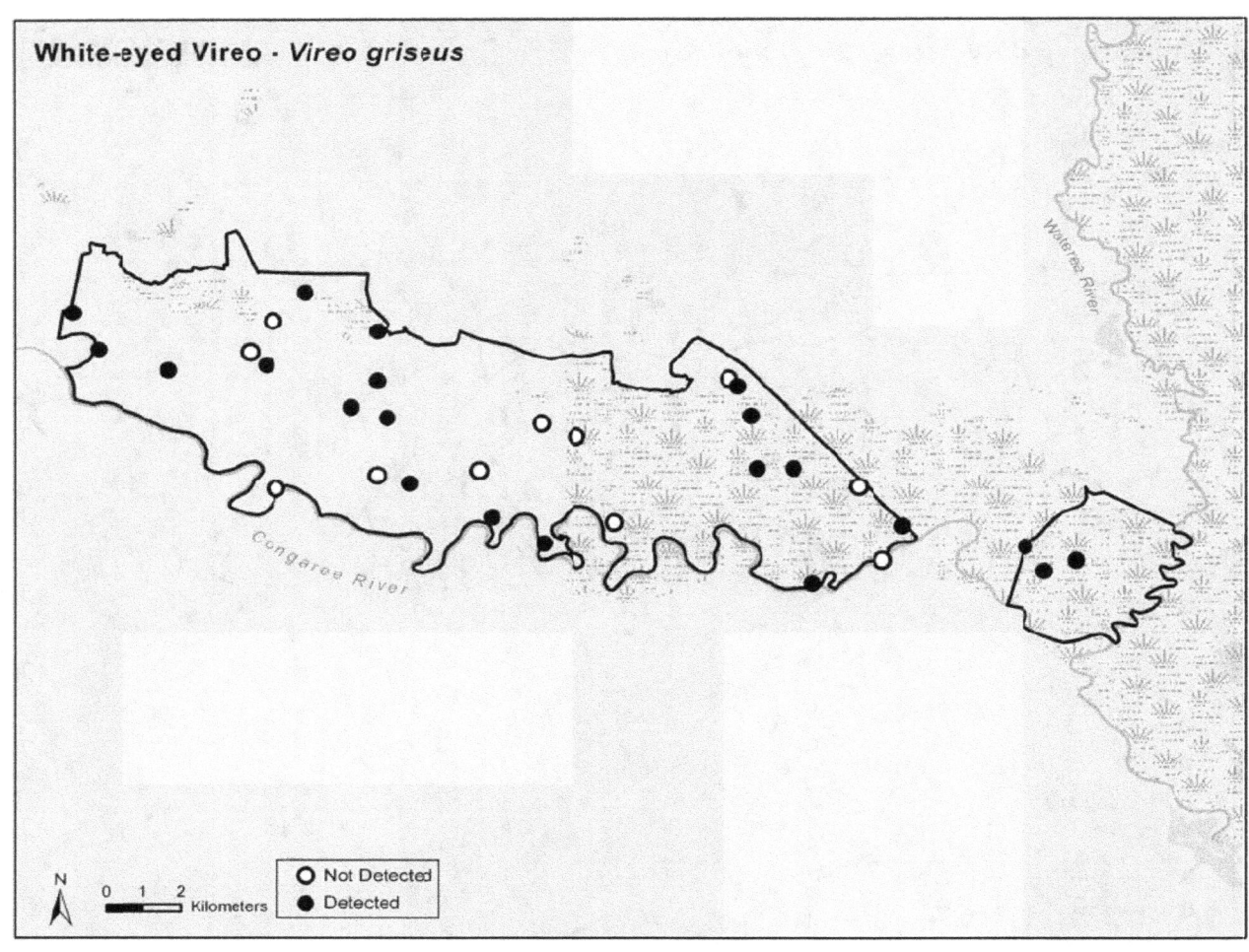

Figure D-61. Sampling locations where White-eyed Vireo (*Vireo griseus*) was detected at CONG, 2009. ● = detected, ○ = not detected.

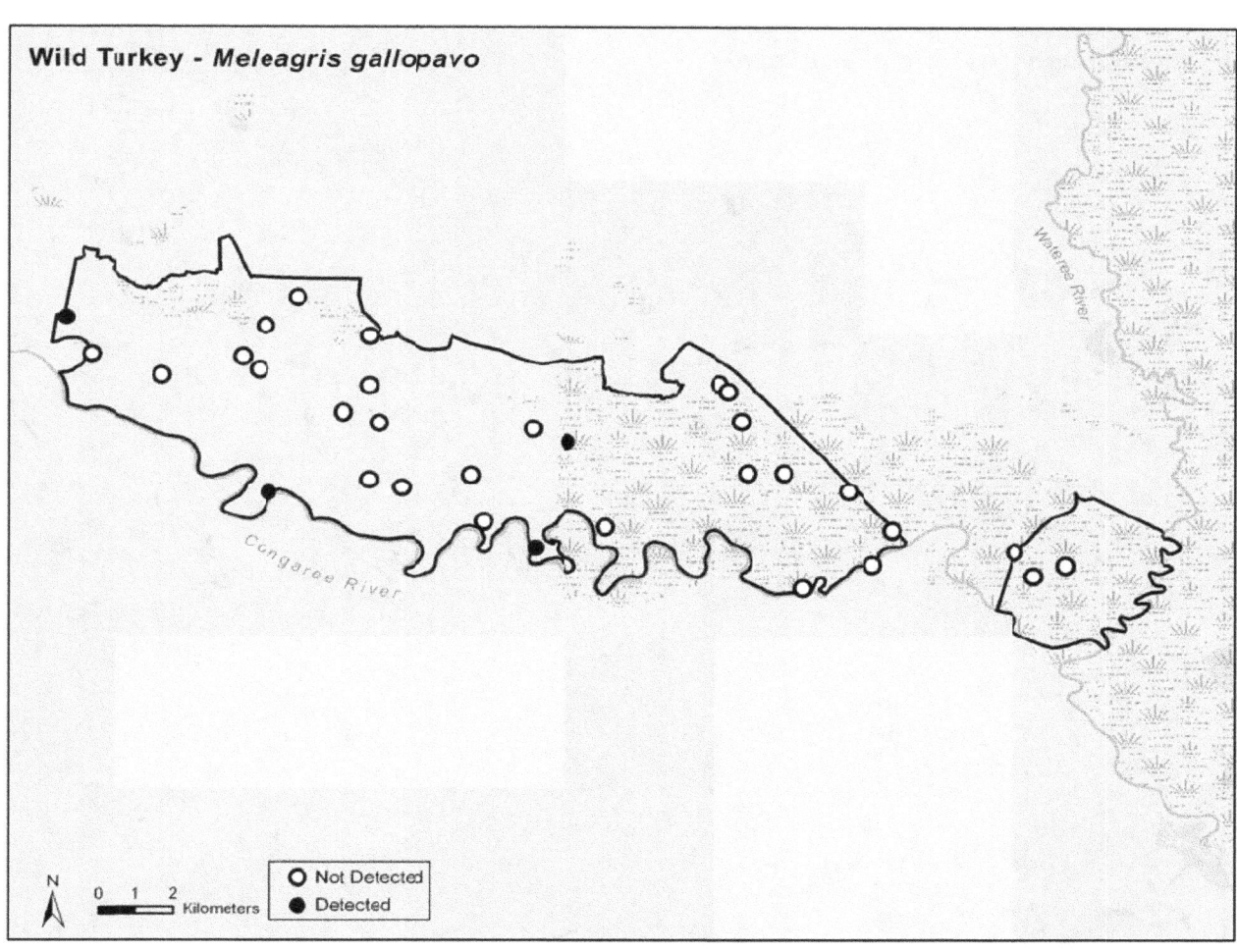

Figure D-62. Sampling locations where Wild Turkey (*Melea ris gallopavo*) was detected at CONG, 2009.
● = detected, ○ = not detected.

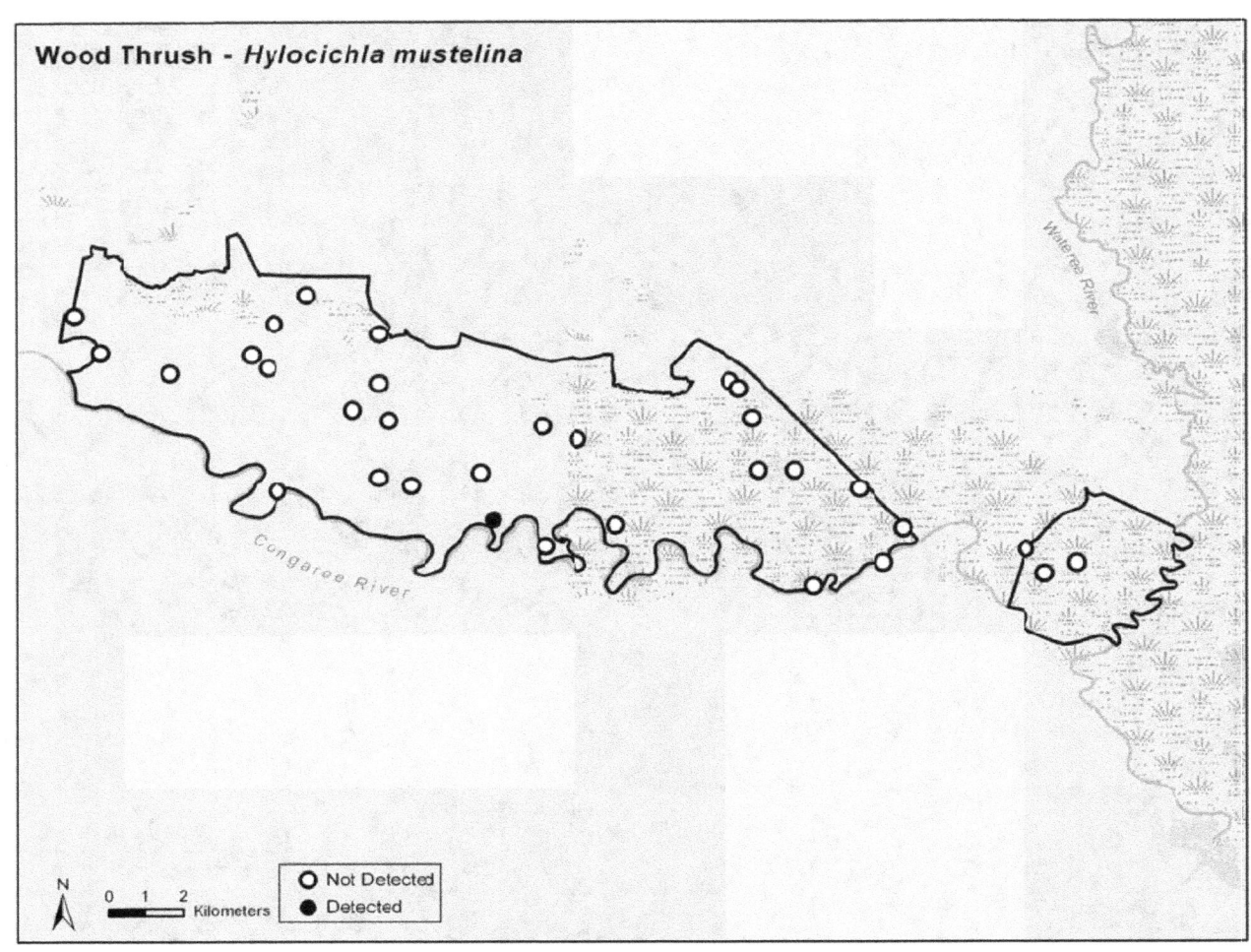

Figure D-63. Sampling locations where Wood Thrush (*Hylo ichla mustelina*) was detected at CONG, 2009. ● = detected, ○ = not detected.

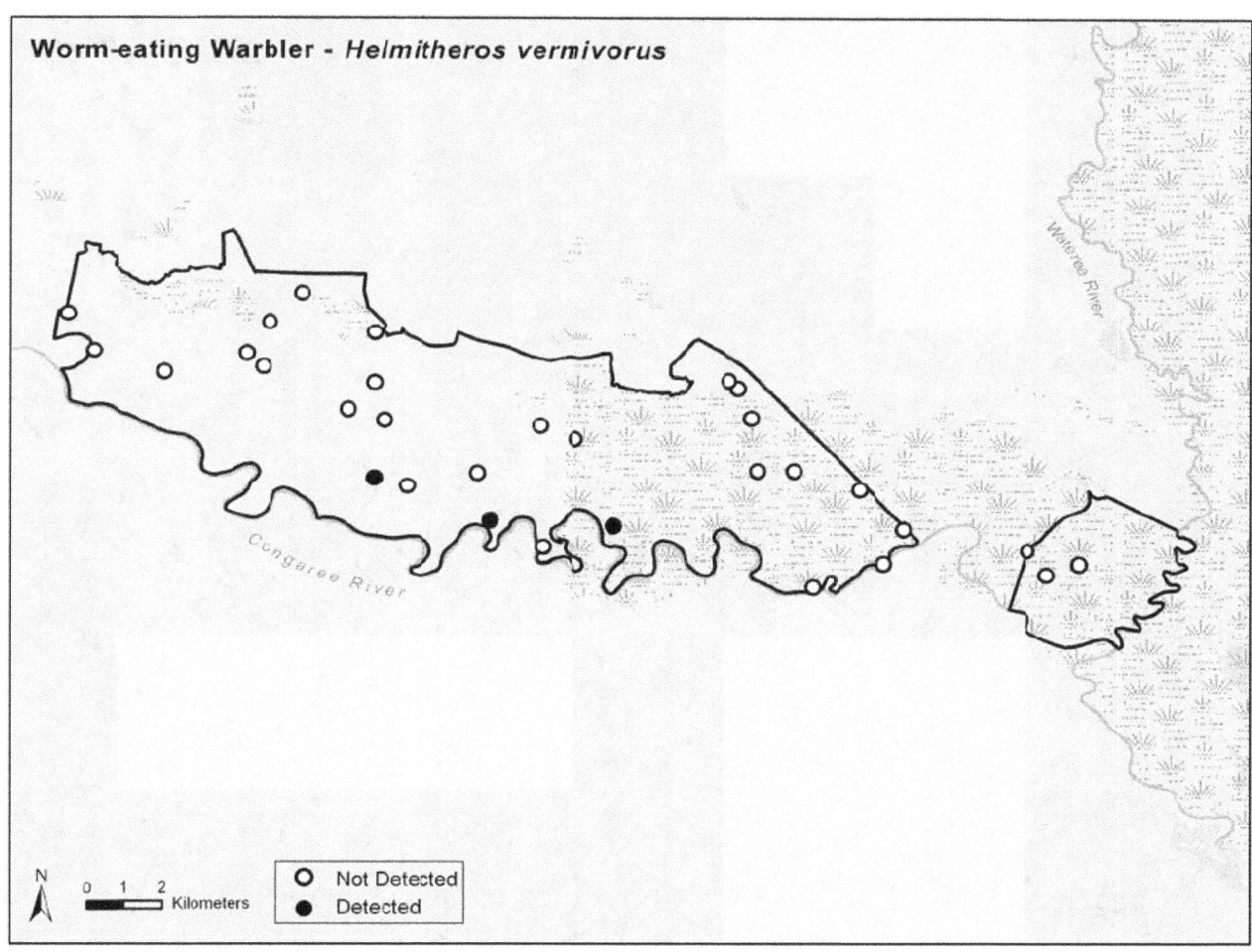

Figure D-64. Sampling locations where Worm-eating Warbler (*Helmitheros vermivorus*) was detected at CONG, 2009. ● = detected, ○ = not detected.

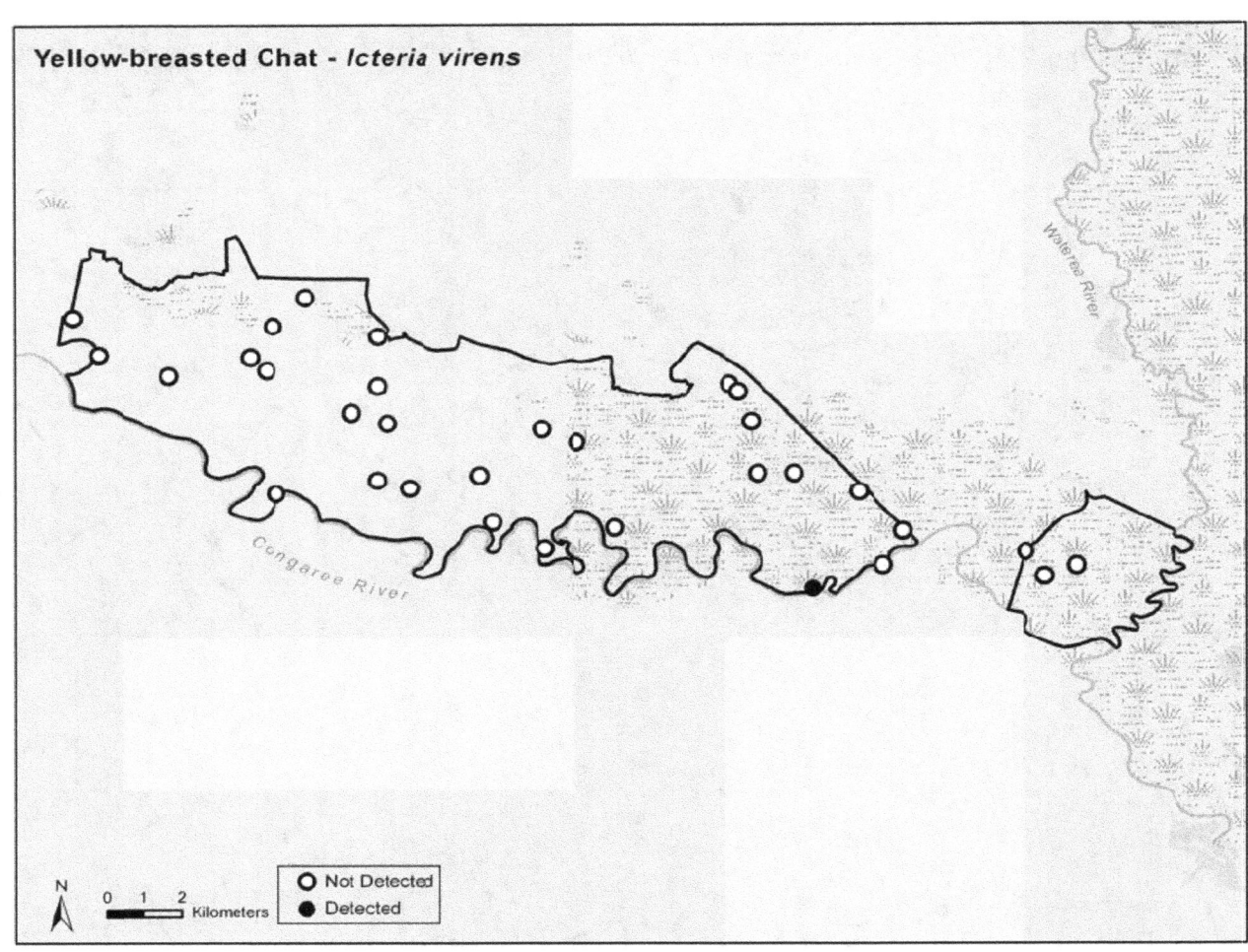

Figure D-65. Sampling locations where Yellow-breasted Ch t (*Icteria virens*)was detected at CONG, 2009. ● = detected, ○ = not detected.

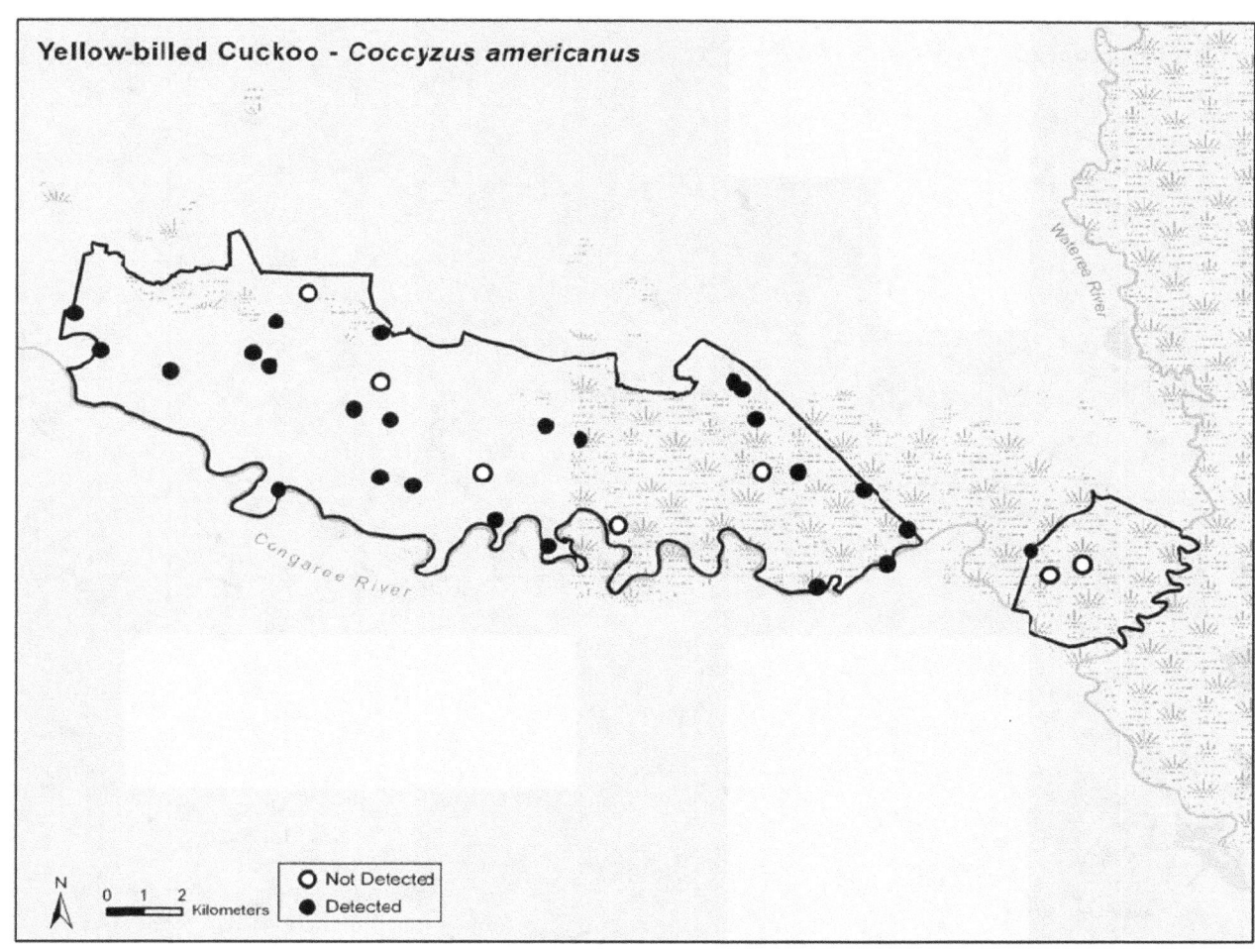

Figure D-66. Sampling locations where Yellow-billed Cucko ̫ (*Coccyzus americanus*) was detected at CONG, 2009. ● = det ̫cted, ○ = not detected.

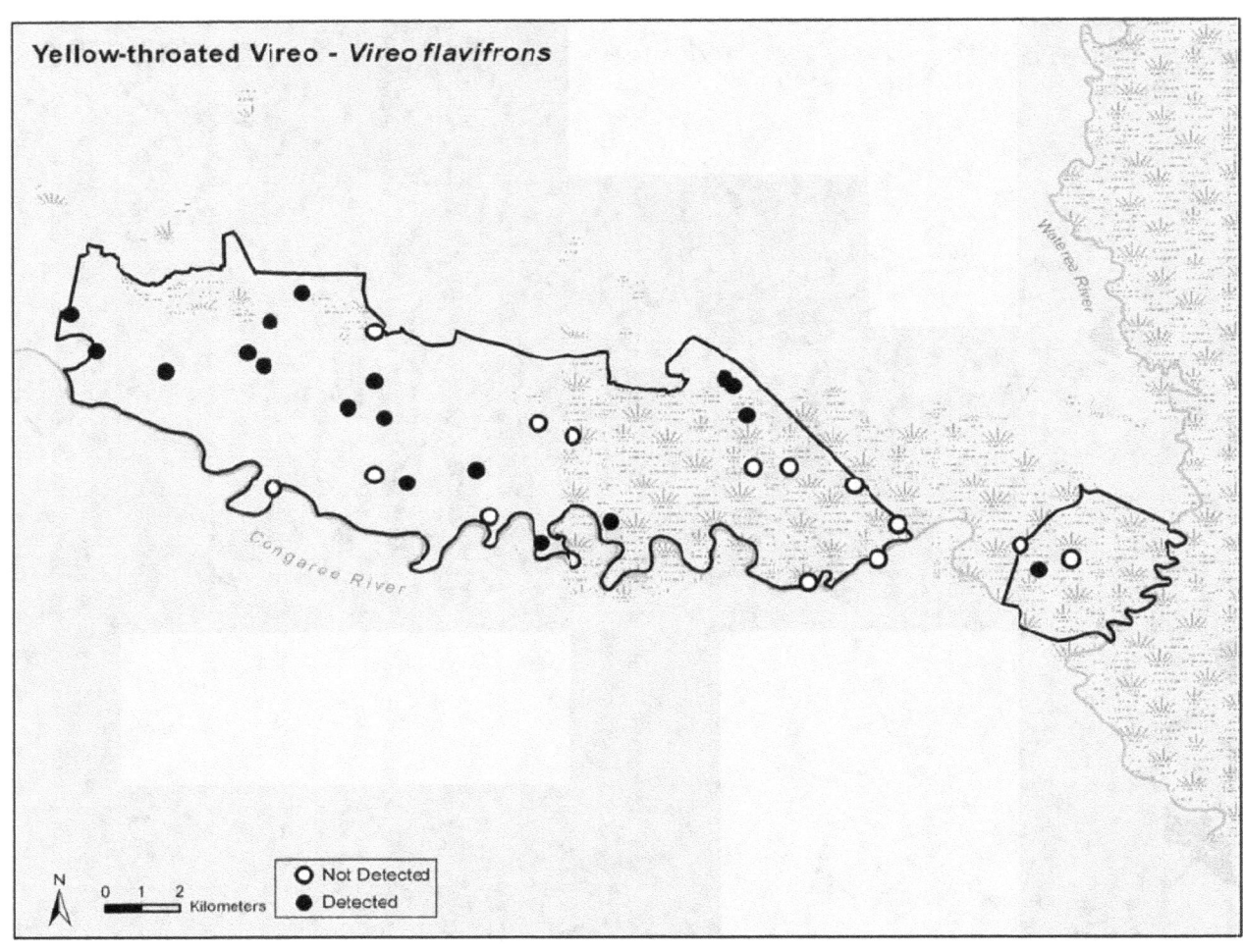

Figure **D-67.** Samplin g locations where Yellow-throated Vire › (*Vireo flavifrons*) was detected at CONG, 2009. ● = detected, ○ = not detected.

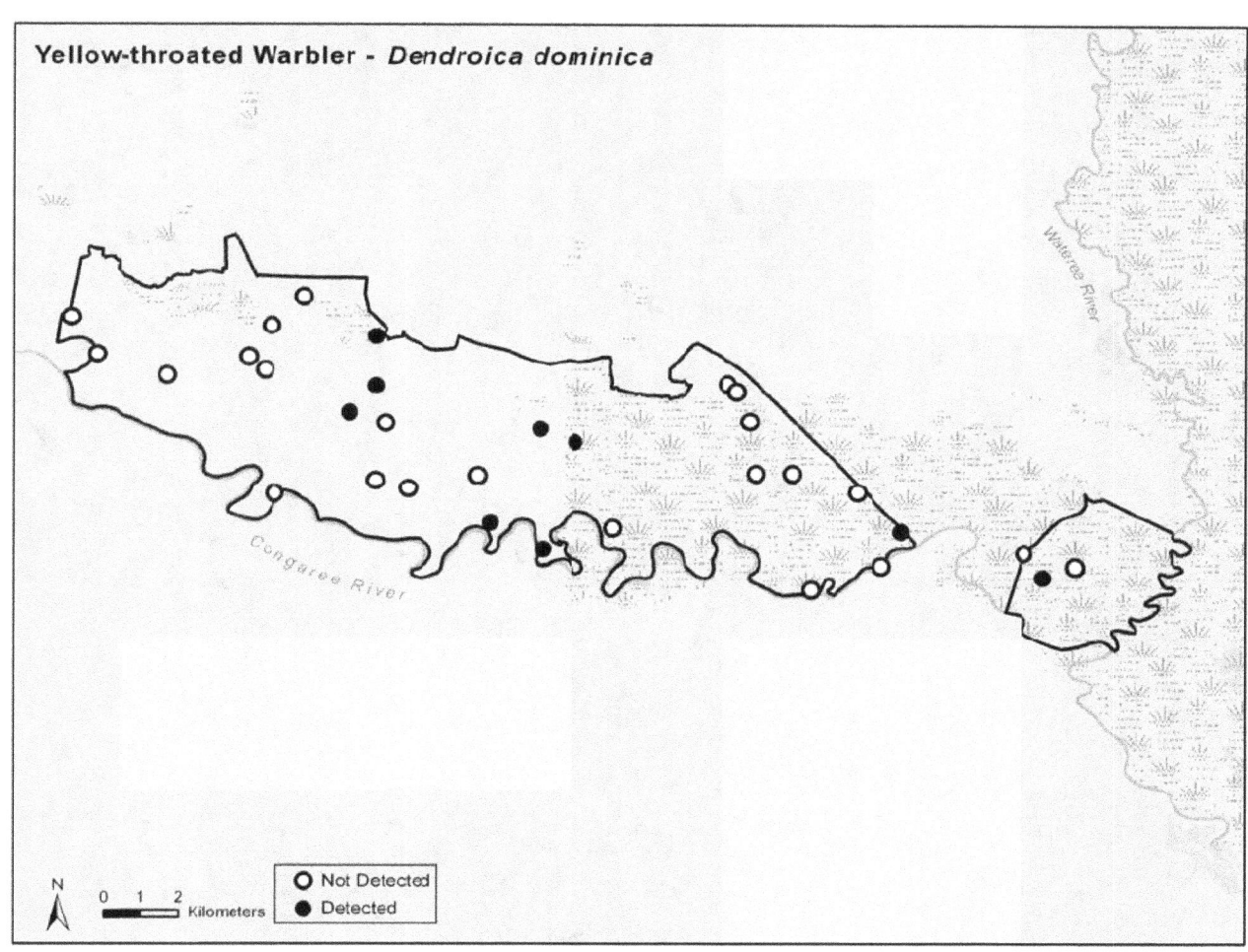

Figure **D-68.** Sampling locations where Yellow-throated Warbler (*Dendroica dominica*) was detected at CONG, 2009. ● = detected, ○ = not detected.